Sustainable Living, Minimalism, and Zero Waste

A Beginner's Guide to a Decluttered Home and Habits to Save the Planet

B. R. Pohl

Table of Contents

Acknowledgements

I would like to thank several people who made this book possible. First, to Kate Wilder for her contributions, including research, and drawing upon her wealth of knowledge on eco-living, her wise counsel, thoughtful organization, and editing contributions.

To my wife Nicka for her encouragement and editing. To my children: David, Laura, and Charlotte for allowing me the time to bring this important message to fruition. And finally, to my dad for content, research, and his continuous support for me in all my endeavors.

Introduction

Shopping has never been easier. Whatever you want is available at the click of a button, be it an essential grocery item or something frivolous that caught your eye online. Particularly since the COVID pandemic hit, online shopping has become more than a convenience. It's turned us into human versions of Pavlov's dog, hitting the "buy now" button to bring rewards: The delivery of umpteen cardboard boxes just for you.

But what if I told you, that every time you hit that addictive "buy now" button, you could be signing the death warrant of an endangered North Atlantic right whale? If that sounds far-fetched, imagine for a moment how the goods you buy reach you. Many are produced in distant lands—like the Far East—and are transported in massive container ships across thousands of miles of ocean to U.S. ports. On the way, these huge vessels encounter a variety of ocean wildlife, including—you guessed it—North Atlantic right whales. One of their primary threats are collisions with commercial vessels like container ships. And that's only one consequence of our consumerist lifestyles.

The proliferation of plastic waste is another. Back in 1997, Captain Charles Moore sailed from Hawaii to southern California (Plastic Soup, n.d.). Miles from land in the Pacific Ocean, he spotted pieces of plastic floating past his boat. He'd actually encountered an environmental disaster—plastic that had broken down into even smaller particles and was present throughout the water column. He called this "plastic soup" (Plastic Soup, n.d.). And, in case you're wondering, plastic is now so prevalent that we're ingesting the equivalent of a credit card every week—around five and a half pounds in a year ("In Pictures: How Much Plastic Are You Eating?," 2020).

You've probably heard about the maritime disaster off Sri Lanka in May 2021, when the *X-Press Pearl* container ship caught fire and sank (McVeigh, 2021). Authorities feared a massive oil spill, as well as other fallout because the vessel was carrying hazardous substances, including nitric acid, caustic soda, and methanol. But the worst hazard, it turns out, wasn't classified "hazardous" at all, yet it continues to have a devastating impact.

The ship was carrying eighty-seven containers of nurdles, lentil-sized plastic pellets that form the basis of a multitude of plastic products, ranging from single-use bottles to toys (McVeigh,

2021). In November 2021, *The Guardian* newspaper reported that billions of nurdles were washing up on the Sri Lankan coast, and were expected to foul regional coastlines too. In some places, the nurdles were up to two meters thick, and were being found in the mouths of fish and the bodies of dead dolphins. It was arguably the biggest plastic spill in history (McVeigh, 2021). If you're using and buying plastic products—and let's face it, nearly all of us are—then you're complicit in these and other plastic disasters.

What about paper? Even in this online age, we still use plenty of it—for fliers, receipts, sticky notes, newsprint, school books, crafts, and much more. The average U.S. office worker uses 10,000 sheets of paper a year, and about a quarter of that gets trashed (O'Mara, 2021). Paper and cardboard are often considered environmentally-friendly options, partly because they're recyclable. They can be reused (so don't ditch those cardboard boxes your online purchases were packed in), and may even be added to your compost heap, if you have one.

What you probably don't know about paper is that as much as 14% of global deforestation is caused solely by our demand for wood pulp for paper. That equates to 4.1 million hectares (10.13 million acres) of forest disappearing every year (Paper on the Rocks, n.d.).

There's no getting away from it: We live in a consumer culture. In fact, our economy is built on consumerism, with consumer spending accounting for a whopping 69% of the U.S. economy (Cox, 2021).

And your online shopping with its promise of "free" returns? Turns out they're not so free—for the biosphere anyway. In the U.S. alone, customers return around 3.5 billion products purchased online, only 20% of which are actually defective (Constable, n.d.). This creates a headache for suppliers, as these returns aren't the same as damaged products. While some resell the items cheaply to discount outlets, many simply truck these unused products to landfill, creating a massive mountain of waste. But you don't actually see that happening, so you continue to order online and return your purchases. After all, out of sight is out of mind.

Landfills perfectly illustrate this concept. Located far from suburbia and shopping malls, they are dreadful places. If you've ever visited one, you'll know what I mean: the overpowering stench of decay; the choking dust kicked up by dump trucks and the bulldozers that move the trash; squawking birds fighting over scraps; and ragged waste pickers scratching through the garbage for recyclables like aluminum soda cans.

These places expose the ugly truth of affluent modern civilization, like bones beneath the skin. They are where its trappings go to die. Besides organic refuse such as garden clippings or food waste, chemical-laden waste like plastic and electronics break down when exposed to the elements, combining with water to create a toxic brew that leaches into the ground, poisoning the soil and perhaps even the groundwater. Landfills are the byproduct of our consumer culture.

Humanity's waste is reaching epic proportions. Landfill space in the U.S.—and elsewhere—is filling up fast. As recently as 2018, the 2,000 landfills that take most of the nation's trash were already approaching full capacity (McCarthy, 2018). The situation worsened after China refused to take recyclable waste from Western nations, including the U.S.

The U.S. produces a staggering 268 million tons of waste every year, about 140 million tons of which goes to landfills. The average American now generates around 4 1/2 pounds of trash daily, as opposed to the global average of just over 1 1/2 pounds per day (McDonald, 2022).

Food tops the list of items that Americans throw away, accounting for almost 22% of landfill trash. This is closely followed by plastics, at just over 19%, and paper, at 13% (McDonald, 2022). Other significant landfill items include metals, wood, textiles, yard debris, glass, rubber or leather, and miscellaneous items. Products and packaging account for 71% of the waste stream, of which packaging makes up 26% (McDonald, 2022).

Modern civilization has advanced in a whirlwind of consumption. It's not enough to have a smartphone; it needs to be upgraded every year or two so that you can keep up with the latest technology.

Our lifestyles have changed too. While your grandmother would probably have packed homemade snacks for road trips, often including a flask of boiling water for hot drinks during cold weather, you're more likely to stop at a fast food restaurant or get takeout. Unfortunately, these meals come with a side serving of plastic ranging from styrofoam containers and plastic-lined cups to plastic cutlery and sauce packets.

The trouble with most of this plastic is that it's "single use." In other words, it's only intended to be used once. However, it may remain intact in the environment for years after it's discarded.

Planned Obsolescence

My friend's parents had a refrigerator that they bought with some of their wedding money in the mid-1960s. When her father died, after 36 years of marriage, the appliance was still going strong. Her mom once boasted that the only maintenance it had ever needed was to replace the inside light bulb. Twelve years later, when her mother left the city where she was living to move to a country town, that refrigerator was still going strong. It had never seen a repairman, and had never been serviced. As her mother used to say, "They don't make refrigerators like this anymore!"

Today, that's truer than ever. Many things in our modern world once lasted much longer: diapers, cameras, cigarette lighters, handheld razors, and more. These and countless other items have deliberately become disposable by design. Manufacturers call this "planned obsolescence"—a clever business ploy that ensures that, when something quickly wears out, or has been used once, consumers need to buy another. This means that producers can sell more products each year, improving their bottom lines to the delight of their shareholders. Mass production of lower quality products also means that cheaper materials can be used—increasing profits for manufacturers.

Sometimes the approach can be quite subtle. Take video games, for example. Many now have a definite end. To play the next installment, another game has to be purchased. Software manufacturers withdraw their support for operating systems or programs that still work, forcing users to buy upgrades. New cars and smartphones entice buyers by offering improved models, which are better looking and include more features.

Unfortunately, "planned obsolescence" has become so much a part of modern life that most consumers no longer notice it. Let's face it: It's exceedingly rare to find groups campaigning for quality products with a longer lifespan.

The Price of Consumption

The BBC's two-part series *The Party's Over: How the West Went Bust* chronicles how, over three decades, Western nations borrowed excessively to feed consumption rather than investment. Production declined and factories closed, outsourcing their production to the Far East, which experienced an economic boom. Individuals became severely over-indebted, just to keep up with the proverbial Joneses, while Far Eastern nationals saved a significant portion of their earnings. Governments borrowed to shore up banking institutions where board members enjoyed billionaire lifestyles and cozied up to officials. This gave rise to a massive debt problem, affecting all members of society and governments across much of the Western world. The financial crash of 2008 sounded the alarm, yet our consumerist lifestyles and business models persist (DocuWiki, 2022).

But the ripple effects of rampant consumerism are not confined to economics or personal finances. The constant production of new and often unnecessary products uses vast amounts of raw materials, such as minerals, crops, wood and other plant derivatives, animal products, and so on. This is taking a huge toll on planetary resources, which not only sustain human lives and the world economy, but ensures the continuation of all life on Earth. Cheap manufacturing processes are causing higher pollution loads, compromising the soil, air, and water that all life depends on.

What Can You Do?

Reading environmental publications or watching television programs about the state of the planet is likely to engender feelings of hopelessness. The problem seems so insurmountable, one might as well be climbing Everest without any preparation. However, when acting collectively, individuals can make a difference.

Essentially, we as consumers need to think twice before we buy—or click the "buy now" button. How long will we use the item? Do we really need it? What is its environmental footprint likely to be? Can it be repaired or recycled if it breaks?

One thing I discovered when applying this principle to smart phones is that many will last long beyond the end of fixed-term contracts, where service providers encourage you to buy the latest, more sophisticated one, and keep you coming back to them year after year, contract after contract.

In this book, you'll find out how to live more sustainably, with practical hints, tips, and swaps. Reduce your waste stream, so less goes to landfill, and more things are recycled, repurposed or reused. You'll also discover how consumerism affects the planet and our lives. Reading this book will empower you to make a difference as an individual, reducing your personal planetary footprint.

Chapter 1:
Cultivating a Sustainable Lifestyle—What Does It Mean?

It's the tail end of a day at the end of winter. The grass is tawny gold, and the bare skeletons of the trees are etched against a cobalt sky. Pecan trees are still holding nuts in the folds of their outer shells, and some birds are already building nests in the branches, anticipating spring. The sun drops low over the hills as I wander down a dirt path to a vegetable garden, where clusters of produce and herbs hug the good, dark earth. In a corner is a compost heap, covered with autumn leaves. A rain tank rests at the edge of a roofline, ready to catch the rain when it comes. A flock of white geese feeds in a field, bright white in the short grass. Someone opens a gate, and the geese stream toward a barn, wings flapping like earth angels. Treasured memorabilia from another time adorn the walls, and native succulents bloom in rustic stone pots. There's a certain timelessness that comes with sustainable living, as you return to a simpler, more satisfying way of life, one that's not dominated by consumption, but enables you to dally among the wildflowers and get in touch with your wild side.

We talk of sighting rare wild birds, installing solar on our properties, cooking from scratch, growing vegetables and plants, and keeping cattle and chickens. We talk of our hopes and dreams as the sun sinks behind the hills, and the first evening chill creeps in. We don't consider ourselves eco-warriors, but we're all concerned with becoming more independent, living lightly on the planet, and making a difference. So what, exactly, is "sustainable living?"

There are many terms that could be used to describe the adoption of a more planet-friendly, eco-conscious lifestyle. For instance, you have likely heard of sustainable living, zero-waste living, and minimalism. Although all are valid, these terms are often used interchangeably. If you are relatively new to the concept of sustainability, this can be confusing. Let's take a look at some commonly used terms and what they actually mean.

Sustainable Living Explained

Sustainable living may be defined as "meeting our own needs without compromising the ability of future generations to meet their needs." This definition was coined by the World Commission on Environment and Development, formed in 1983, and headed by Norwegian prime minister Gro Brundtland (University of Alberta, 2013). Later known as the Brundtland

Commission, it authored a report entitled *Our Common Future*, one of the first documents to define sustainability in concrete terms.

Although it's gaining more ground these days, the concept is actually not a new idea. It has its roots in diverse practices, including social justice, conservation, internationalism, and several other ideologies. By the end of the twentieth century, these ideas had coalesced in the sustainability movement (University of Alberta, 2013).

Sustainable living is a practical way of life that aims to reduce one's personal, societal, and environmental impact by making positive changes to one's lifestyle. The idea is that these changes will help counteract negative scenarios such as climate change, for example, by reducing one's "carbon footprint" (the amount of carbon generated by everyday activities such as using electricity, driving vehicles, or shopping). Those who embrace sustainable living work actively to reduce their use of planetary resources, and find ways of interacting with the natural environment without harming or degrading it.

Natural resources aside, people also have social and economic needs, so sustainability is about more than environmentalism. In fact, the three so-called "pillars" of sustainability are environment, economy, and society. While the pillars can stand alone, their convergence is considered to be true sustainability.

Environmental Sustainability

Sustainable living aims to maintain ecological integrity, working toward environmental equilibrium. People consume natural resources at a rate where they are able to be replenished, thereby maintaining the balance of Earth systems. This may be referred to as net zero living. Don't take from the Earth more than you need.

Economic Sustainability

This means that all human communities have access to the resources they require to meet their needs. Communities retain their independence, while economic systems are intact and inclusive, ensuring secure livelihoods.

Social Sustainability

All people have human rights, and everyone is able to access basic necessities—enough to ensure that their families and communities are healthy and secure. Leaders respect personal, labor, and cultural rights, and protect community members from discrimination.

While environmentalists may be inclined to focus on this aspect to the exclusion of the others, ignoring social and economic realities may result in the collapse of environmental sustainability. Nevertheless, it's important to remember that all human needs should be met within the parameters of planetary resources. We need to be careful not to exert too much pressure on the Earth's life support systems, upon which we, and all life, depend. These include things such as a stable climate, fertile soils, and the protective ozone layer.

What is Zero Waste Living?

Those who have joined the zero waste movement have a single aim: to send nothing whatsoever to landfill. That's right. Nothing. The idea behind zero waste is to pare down your needs, reuse as much as possible, send a little to be recycled, and compost anything that doesn't fall into these categories.

Paul Palmer, a chemist from Yale University, founded the Zero Waste Institute in California in the 1970s, thereby starting the movement (Mauch, 2016). He went on to found a company based on this premise, which collected unwanted laboratory chemicals and resold them to scientists and companies. But zero waste lifestyles actually go back much further—to the Great Depression. Consumption patterns then were vastly different: People never wasted anything because they couldn't afford to. Things you needed, such as clothing, were made by someone close to you, or even yourself. They were quality items, not mass produced in the Far East. This trend continued into the 1950s (Kellogg, 2020). There was no circular economy then because things were generally made to last.

Standard grocery items like sugar, flour, and beans were purchased by weight and packed in plain paper bags for shoppers to take home. They weren't labeled either, hence stories of mixing up salt and sugar in baking recipes!

There's another aspect to zero waste, and that's the issue of redefining the current consumerist system. At present, most economies are linear. That means products are created or manufactured, used for a time, and then dumped. No attempt is made to extend the life cycle of the product, reuse component parts, or recycle some elements. The ultimate goal of zero waste is to enable a transition to a circular economy.

In a circular economy, instead of discarding resources, we create a system where they can be reabsorbed. After all, there's no trash in nature. Today's production system tends to be linear:

Resources are mined and used to produce various products, which then become waste when they are disposed of. By contrast, a circular economy keeps materials, products, and services in play for as long as possible. Products, services, and systems are designed to maximize their value and minimize waste. The ultimate goal is to develop products in such a way as to reduce the likelihood of them ending up in landfill at the end of their useful lives. Businesses that supply products and services get the most value out of the natural resources used. Products are designed with the entire life cycle in mind, both reusing and repairing to extend their life, and then reusing components to create new products from the old ones when that is no longer feasible.

While several blogs and articles promote the benefits of recycling—and going zero waste also helps—the crux of the matter is that we can't really recycle our way out of this. This is because there's too much to process because our consumption rates are way too high. In fact, if you consider the three Rs—Reduce, Reuse, Recycle—recycling comes last. This is because recycling is an imperfect solution, relying to a great degree on consumer participation in recycling programs. This is part of the reason why a mere nine percent of plastic is actually recycled in the U.S. (Kellogg, 2020). A lot of recycled items are also contaminated, as they're not properly cleaned before being dumped into recycle bins, and are therefore thrown out when they reach the recycling center.

Central to the idea of zero waste is becoming more mindful as a consumer. Before buying anything, consider whether you really need it. Buy secondhand items before new ones, reuse something that you already have, or buy resusables rather than disposables (e.g. cloth diapers rather than disposable ones). Adopt a "less is more" approach; you don't need several different household cleaners when one will do the job. Remember that every purchase you make—or don't—sends a message about the kind of world you want to live in.

Embracing Minimalism

Popularized by several celebrities—some of whom have even written books about it—minimalism has become trendy. Drawing in those who yearn to live a simpler life with fewer distractions, less technology, and less stuff in general, this lifestyle choice epitomizes "less is more." As a society, we have forgotten that it's the simple things in life that often bring the greatest personal pleasure: spending time with loved ones, cooking, reading, being creative, exercising, or simply doing nothing for a while. Our psyches are overwhelmed, overstimulated, and over-anxious. Excessive clutter and possessions may even elevate our stress levels.

In a nutshell, "a minimalist lifestyle is the process of identifying what is essential in your life, and having the courage to eliminate the rest. When you remove the unnecessary, you free up your time and capacity to focus on the things that really matter" (Ofei, 2022).

While adopting minimalism means that you choose to have fewer material things, it enables you to make the most out of what you already have. Not only that, you become more agile and able to respond to change. You have fewer responsibilities and commitments, and less pressure. Having fewer possessions can, in some ways, provide more flexibility. Moving to a smaller house means having less financial commitment and less maintenance, freeing up time to spend on other, potentially enriching things. Choosing to ditch your car, for instance, can enlarge your world by creating new experiences when you walk, or social opportunities when using public transport. (Many years ago, a friend's work colleague met her future husband while commuting to work on the bus!)

Contrary to popular opinion, becoming a minimalist doesn't mean that you need to throw everything out, take your children out of good schools, or sell your car and your house (although you may decide to do these things in time.). One of the defining traits of minimalists is that they don't buy for the sake of acquiring things. They buy to replace items that have worn out and often buy secondhand. Sometimes, they will buy new things, but only with careful consideration. True minimalists rarely rush out and splurge on impulse. Of course, there are the so-called "extreme minimalists," who insist on owning only a certain number of things. But it's not about numbers; it's about adopting a less cluttered lifestyle, avoiding hyper-consumption, and focusing on the things that really matter to you.

A Common Thread

So what do all these concepts have in common? Let's take single-use plastic bottles, for instance. Zero waste living aims to reduce, or preferably eliminate, unwanted items and food going to landfills. This means that a zero waste enthusiast avoids using— and then throwing away—single-use disposable plastic bottles, as these would likely end up in a landfill somewhere. The zero waste focus is therefore on reducing the volume of packaging waste.

Sustainable living advocates reason that, as plastic breaks down, it releases greenhouse gasses such as methane into the atmosphere. Methane is a primary contributor to global warming and climate change. For this reason, they decide to eliminate as many single-use plastic bottles from their lives as possible. The bottles therefore don't reach the landfill, as they aren't even purchased in the first place.

Minimalists aim to consume less of everything in the interests of having more freedom, peace, clarity, and the time to pursue things they consider important. They might choose to give up their daily soda routine for health reasons, as well as the weekly chore of purchasing, followed by chilling, storing, and ultimately discarding the bottle.

As you can see, in all three cases, these people resolved the issue of single-use plastic bottles going to landfill. Their reasons for doing so differed, but the end result was the same.

Now that you know more about sustainable living, zero waste, and minimalism, let's consider humanity's overall planetary footprint. How much of Earth's natural resources are we using as a species, and is this sustainable?

How Are We Doing?

The Global Footprint Network is an organization that assists companies, organizations, and individuals in establishing how many planetary resources they are using, and how to reduce this. In 2006, they started the Earth Overshoot Day campaign. This marks the day when humanity has used its natural resource budget for the year. From Earth Overshoot Day to the end of the year, we're basically living on ecological credit. The organization says that humanity has been living on credit for some time, and we are now effectively using nearly two planets-worth of resources annually. (Global Footprint Network, 2016). In 2017, for example, humanity used up 173% of the planet's natural resources, as opposed to 119% in 1980 (Taub, 2021).

Some studies indicate that, if everyone lived like the average American, it would take the resources of five Earths to sustain humanity (Center for Sustainable Systems, 2021). Reducing our planetary footprint isn't difficult: It takes forethought and, above all, the desire to change. For example, the average American uses two hundred and forty gallons of water daily, but this can be reduced to forty-eight gallons a day simply by plugging household leaks. With less than 5% of the world's population, the U.S. consumes 16% of global energy resources, and accounts for 15% of the world's Gross Domestic Product (GDP). From 1990–2019, U.S. greenhouse gas emissions increased by 1.8% to 20 metric tons of carbon dioxide equivalent per person, with electricity generation accounting for 25% of this (Center for Sustainable Systems, 2021).

The Global Footprint Network has now started a #MoveTheDate campaign in an endeavor to reduce the natural resources humans are currently using to one Earths-worth of resources a year. That's not as easy as it seems. If the date is moved back by just six days a year, humanity would be using one Earth by 2050. But there's a snag: Reaching the International Panel on Climate Change's (IPCC) 2030 carbon emissions reduction target would take more than those six days, leaving us in deficit once more (Global Footprint Network, 2016). Nevertheless, the campaign has many backers.

What Can You Do?

When looking at the facts, it's easy to become disheartened. What can an individual possibly do to change the trajectory we are on? The task seems so daunting that it's difficult to find a place to start.

Living sustainably includes many other issues related to environmental stewardship, reducing consumption, and enabling sustainable choices. These include clean energy, water use, sustainable food systems, greenhouse gasses and climate change, organic gardening and farming, eco-homes, corporate sustainability, and eco-friendly public policy, to name just a few. So, there's a lot you can do to change the world we live in. There are many green options and choices you can make that will enable you to transition to a more sustainable lifestyle. These are generally referred to as swaps or eco-hacks. Some are easily implemented, while others may require soul-searching and discipline.

Chapter 2:
Pushing the Limits—How Bad Is It Really?

The first—and only—time my friend saw a loggerhead turtle in the ocean, it was almost overcome by trash. Torrential rains had lashed the adjacent inland areas that week, bringing rivers down in flood, and scouring out coastal estuaries. Along with uprooted trees, stray logs, and clumps of vegetation, a tide of human detritus surged into the sea. The turtle swam determinedly through a cornucopia of rubber sandals, discarded tires, misshapen plastic containers, soccer balls, toilet seats, broken chairs, sodden clothing, and plenty else. The volume of trash in the ocean detracted from our offshore excursion, and she spent most of the trip feeling appalled that wild creatures had to live in circumstances like these. And that was before trash-laden beaches dominated the headlines.

Today, sights like these are common, as are beaches so laden with trash that you'd be hard-pressed to find a spot to put up your sun umbrella and build a sandcastle with your children. Beach clean-ups in 2021 in the U.K. revealed that 74% of beach trash consists of plastic and styrofoam (Sky News 2021).

In this chapter, you'll discover just why humans need to reduce our environmental footprint, to live within the limits of our planet, and give all life forms a fighting chance at survival. Sustainable living, as we've mentioned previously, is a vast subject. Here, I'll be focusing on just a few aspects: plastic, paper, electronics, the cosmetics industry, and the fast fashion trend.

Plastic: Here to Stay?

Plastic is made of polymers, sometimes derived from natural substances, but more often from fossil fuels like petroleum. They consist of long chains of atoms, the patterns and length of which make the polymers strong, lightweight, and flexible—all properties of plastic that account for its versatility, durability, and popularity. It's also relatively inexpensive when compared to other options for packaging, storage, and countless other applications.

From today's perspective, it's hard to imagine, but plastic was considered an environmental savior when it was first invented. This was because it could be substituted for finite natural resources threatened with overexploitation, and people were actually encouraged to use more of it! Plastic could be crafted and molded to resemble natural materials like tortoiseshell, ivory, wood, and stone, to name but a few, and could be used as a replacement. Not only that, it was believed that plastic would free humanity from the constraints of using only natural materials for our needs.

So how did this happen? Let's consider the history of plastic in this context. John Hyatt developed the first plastic-like material in 1869, when he entered a competition to create a substitute for ivory (Science History Institute, 2016). He treated cellulose from cotton fiber with camphor. The resulting compound could be molded into different shapes, and crafted to look like natural materials.

Leo Baekeland invented Bakelite in 1907 (Science History Institute, 2016). This was the first completely synthetic plastic, and was intended to replace shellac as an electrical insulator at a time when the U.S. was undergoing widespread electrification. Bakelite's other properties included durability, heat resistance, and its suitability for mechanical mass production. It could be molded into virtually anything.

Plastic use boomed during World War II, when U.S. production increased by a staggering 300% (Science History Institute, 2016). This was partly because nylon was invented and used to make parachutes, body armor, ropes, helmet liners, and much more.

The plastic revolution continued after the war and the Great Depression. Yet again, it was promoted as an environmentally-friendly alternative to diminishing natural resources. But not everyone was so altruistic. There were those who envisaged increased wealth-generating opportunities based on an inexpensive, safe, and sanitary substance that could be shaped to satisfy virtually any human need.

All good things come to an end and, by the early 1970s, humanity's love affair with plastic had begun to reveal its dark side. With the dawn of environmentalism, people were becoming uneasy about the specter of plastic waste—and with good reason (Science History Institute, 2016). Since the 1950s, a stupendous 9.14 billion tons has been produced, with the current annual manufacture being around 380 million metric tons (EDN Staff, 2022).

Single-Use Plastic

Around ½ of all the plastic produced is used to make single-use products like plastic bottles, which we use at the rate of 1.2 million a minute (EDN Staff, 2022). Single-use plastic bottles are used worldwide, mostly for packaging bottled water and soft drinks. In a sense, the bottles that hold things like body washes, shampoo, and cleaning products are also single-use in that many are not made from recyclable plastic, and are discarded once the product inside is finished.

In 2021, around 583 billion plastic bottles were produced, about 100 million up from 5 years ago. The amount of single-use plastics has practically doubled since the start of the COVID pandemic, most of it attributable to takeout orders (EDN Staff, 2022). Not only that, almost 2.5 million plastic bottles and other containers are thrown out every year without being recycled (Hutchings, 2018).

Plastic items last an incredibly long time in the environment, much longer than they are used for, and sometimes way longer than your lifetime on this planet. Here's an indication of how long certain everyday plastic items take to disappear:

- Plastic shopping bags pose one of the greatest threats to marine life, although they represent a relatively small amount of our plastic waste. They take around 20 years to biodegrade but, during that time, they tend to break up into even smaller pieces, which are hazardous to marine life.
- Takeaway coffee cups take around 30 years to break down due to the plastic membrane inside.

- Although you'll only use a plastic straw for as long as it takes to finish your soft drink, they take about 2 centuries to disappear completely!

- Six-pack plastic rings take even longer, a staggering 400 years. In that time, they can severely impact marine life, which tends to become entangled in them if they end up in the ocean.

- There's been a lot of focus in recent years on single-use plastic bottles, as they make up a significant amount of our trash. One bottle takes about 450 years to decompose.

- Plastic cups are wonderfully durable, but they're also very resistant to breaking down if they're thrown away. They take the same time to biodegrade as single-use plastic bottles.

- Disposable diapers don't break down very well when they're buried in landfills, as they need sunlight and oxygen to aid decomposition. Even in ideal conditions, they take 500 years to break down. That's a good reason to switch to cloth diapers or other eco-friendly alternatives.

- Coffee pods are every coffee drinker's favorite kitchen gadget—but did you know that those tiny cups take over 500 years to break down? While some manufacturers are now producing recyclable coffee pods, you might want to rethink the way you get your caffeine fix.

- We all use toothbrushes, and both the handle and bristles are made of plastic; in fact, 3.5 billion are sold globally every year. When they need replacing, we simply dump them in the trash and buy another. This seemingly insignificant addition to the plastic waste stream takes around 500 years to break down (that's a whopping five centuries).

(World Wildlife Fund, Australia, 2021).

A Word About Packaging

Whenever you buy anything, consider the packaging. Packaging such as cardboard boxes and paper can be reused, recycled, or even composted. However, a significant amount of packaging is actually made of plastic, mainly because it's versatile and cheap.

Take bubble wrap, for instance. Invented in the 1950s, it has become popular for packaging fragile or breakable items, so much so that 240,000 miles of it are produced annually in the U.K. alone (Hall, 2021). It is made of low-density polyethylene, a low grade plastic. When discarded in a landfill, it can take 500 years to fully decompose (Hall, 2021). Bubble wrap can, however, be recycled, and is then turned into things like garbage bags, flooring, furniture, or pipes. Alternatives to bubble wrap include using old sheets, towels and newspapers, shredded paper, hay or straw, or corrugated cardboard packaging.

Paper—a Tree Hugger's Nightmare

Paper is everywhere, and we really don't think too much about it. Most of us use paper every day, whether at work or at home, when we shop, or even for leisure activities. Globally, we used a stupendous amount; just under 440 million tons of paper and paperboard in 2020, a figure that's expected to jump to 513 million metric tons by 2031. The U.S. used to be the world's biggest producer, but China has taken the honors since the mid-2000s (Tiseo, 2022). It takes around 24 trees to produce just over a ton (220,000 sheets) of paper (Law, 2021),

Paper has actually been with us for millenia. The Egyptians made the first paper from papyrus reeds. This was replaced by beeswax-covered wooden tablets, which were used by the ancient Egyptians, Greeks, and Romans. The Romans were the first to produce books made from papyrus. The Chinese developed hemp paper, something we're returning to today. Finally, the Europeans got in on the act, producing paper from linen and cotton rags. This really took off; the first cotton paper mill opened in 1690 in the American colonies (Law, 2021). However, cotton paper became so popular that eventually there weren't enough rags available, and people started using wood pulp to make paper.

We all use incredible amounts of toilet paper—but we rarely consider the environmental cost of this everyday staple. China and the U.S. use the most; in the latter, the average person uses around 141 rolls annually, which means that 31 million trees need to be felled, assuming that one tree produces 1,500 rolls. The U.K. uses slightly less, at around 127 rolls a year, requiring 5.7 million trees to supply demand (Alex, 2022).

If you live in North America, buying and using this everyday item is likely contributing to the destruction of Canada's boreal forests, one of the region's most fundamental ecosystems. Over a million acres are felled every year for toilet paper alone, emitting 26 million metric tons of carbon dioxide, and leaving 90% of the disturbed land exhausted (Alex, 2022). A significant amount of Canada's wood pulp and paper products are exported to the U.S.

Toilet paper is made from virgin fibers, recycled fibers, or both. Virgin fibers are where the issue lies: These come from trees cut down specifically for producing new paper, while recycled fibers are generated from old paper products. At least 80% of U.S. paper mills use recycled material to make their products (Montanari, 2021).

In some cases, the environmental destruction is offset by harvesting trees from commercial plantations. Although this may, in a sense, "save" old-growth forests from being turned into products like toilet paper, timber plantations are not necessarily the answer. They often have a negative impact on biodiversity, communities, and even local economies. The U.N. Food and Agricultural Organization predicted in 2012 that between 40–90 million hectares (98–222 million acres) of monoculture plantations would be planted by 2030 (Rojas, 2012).

Forest vs Plantation: What's the Difference?

Plantations are not forests. A forest is a complex, biodiverse, and self-generating system, including soil, water, a microclimate, and numerous different plants and animals. The value of true forests is immeasurable, as they host more than 70% of land-based biodiversity (Rojas, 2012). They are thus critical for the survival of both humans and the planet. Close to two billion people rely on forests directly or indirectly, including millions of indigenous peoples (Rojas, 2012).

By contrast, monoculture plantations have minimal biodiversity, and need constant intervention to remain productive. This includes the application of fertilizers, pesticides, and herbicides. Local communities tend to lose land and resources to such plantations. There's another problem with plantations: land grabbing. International corporations establish plantations in developing countries, expanding gradually until their operations cover vast tracts of land. This means that they gain control of, and access to, land and resources. Communities who refuse to endorse plantation developments are often threatened. Ironically, massive plantations may even replace forests in some cases, thereby causing deforestation. There are relatively few cases where plantations are established on degraded land.

Other Impacts of Paper

Logging isn't the only potentially detrimental aspect of papermaking. After logs are chipped, they are mixed with chemicals to break down the lignin (a natural compound that confers rigidity to plants), and expose the soft pulp. The leftover mixture is known as "black liquor." While some papermakers recover this and use it to generate energy for the paper mill, others do not, and these harmful chemicals may then enter the natural environment.

The pulp is then treated with chlorine bleach to whiten it, but this can harm aquatic life. For this reason, some paper mills no longer use it, or need to comply with laws prohibiting its use. Buying chlorine-free paper discourages the use of chlorine bleach, which is important, especially when you consider that mills use around 17,000 gallons of water per metric ton of paper produced (Montanari, 2021). If chlorine has not been used, part of this water may be recycled.

The good news is that recycling rates for paper products in the U.S. are much higher than those for plastic at almost 66% (Montanari, 2021).

Unnatural Beauty: Cosmetics and Personal Care Products

Your face is just a face, isn't it? Not to the cosmetics and personal care industry. It treats the different parts of your face as separate entities in the bid to sell you more products, and the average woman uses at least 16 facial products alone (Rai, 2019). And that's not all. Behind the sophisticated packaging, gorgeous models, promises of youthful elixirs, heady fragrances, and squeaky-clean personal care, lie many dirty secrets. These include toxic chemicals—often hidden behind epithets such as "natural," "pure," or "organic"—mountains of appealing but hard-to-recycle packaging, unsustainable ingredients, animal testing, high water use, and transport emissions. The industry's products are contributing to deforestation, coral bleaching, and climate change.

Not Just Skin Deep

The beauty industry has been widely criticized for its use of toxic chemicals. Parabens, plasticizers, formaldehyde, beta hydroxy acid (BHA), coal tar, and even pesticides are found in the personal care products and cosmetics we use regularly. But it's not only humans that are affected by these detrimental substances. The chemicals don't stay on our bodies; they leach into the natural environment. A good example is oxybenzone, a common sunscreen ingredient. This chemical leads to coral bleaching, as it disrupts the coral's reproductive cycle. That's probably not surprising, when you consider that we unleash 17,000 tons of sunscreen on coral reefs every year (Young, 2022). In fact, it's gotten so bad that sunscreens have been banned from Thailand's marine parks, as well as the state of Hawaii, and Palau Island in the Pacific Ocean.

Packaging Waste

The beauty industry is known for its attractive, detailed packaging, which is as much part of brand identity as logos and unique formulations. Cosmetics come with plenty of extraneous packaging, which accounts for as much as 70% of the industry's waste—as many as 120 billion units a year are discarded by consumers (Okafor, 2021).

Adding to the problem, the packaging tends to mix materials together, which makes recycling difficult, if not impossible. This means that 56% of British people don't recycle their shampoo and shower gel bottles because it's too complicated (Okafor, 2021).

While many brands are attempting to clean up their act, investing in solutions such as refillable bottles and jars, and simpler, more recyclable packaging, consumer expectations in some cases need to be revised as well.

Plastic Hiding in Your Personal Care Products

Besides plastic packaging, many personal care products in particular actually contain polyethylene—a type of plastic—as an ingredient. It's often used for microbeads: tiny particles usually found in body scrubs and exfoliants. When you use these products, thousands of microplastics enter your wastewater, ending up in aquatic ecosystems. There, they attract toxins and are swallowed by fish mistaking them for food. You also eat them when you eat contaminated fish. Although the U.S. and U.K. have both banned microbead production, some products still contain them.

Environmentally Destructive Ingredients

The beauty industry uses a startling array of natural resources. Palm oil is one of the most popular ingredients in beauty products, and high demand is leading to the conversion of biodiverse tropical rainforests to oil palm plantations. In fact, your body lotion could be killing orangutans if it contains this cheap, sought-after vegetable oil (although you might not recognize it, as it has as many as 20 different names.). Between 1,000 and 5,000 orangutans are killed on palm oil concessions every year (Young, 2022). Other oils used in products, such as soy, rapeseed, and coconut can also be detrimental if they are not being cultivated sustainably.

Mica, used to add sparkle to beauty products, is found in lipstick and eyeshadow. Mining for the mineral has a slew of negative humanitarian and environmental impacts. As many as 22,000 children, some as young as 4, are obliged to work in the mines, which are mainly situated in extremely poverty-stricken, rural regions in places like Madagascar and India (Cecilia, 2020). The pay is extremely low but so desperate are the inhabitants of these areas that this at least means a steady income. Mica is processed by several intermediaries in different countries, including China, so it's very hard to establish where it was originally mined, and what the social or environmental impacts of the mine were.

Mica is mined in open pits that induce soil erosion and promote sinkholes. These mines could potentially contaminate both ground and surface water, together with the soil. In forested regions, extensive land clearing may be needed to provide access for mica mines. This is leading to deforestation in some places, which has a knock-on effect on the wildlife that live in these forests, as they effectively lose their homes.

Water is a primary ingredient in both cosmetics and personal care products, sometimes listed as "aqua" or "eau" on product labels. However, it's a shrinking natural resource around the world, with almost three billion people already facing water scarcity for at least one month of the year. By 2025, two-thirds of the world's population may be facing water shortages, and the situation for natural systems will become equally dire (World Wildlife Fund, 2022).

Single-Use Products

As with fast food, single use products also increase the beauty industry's waste footprint. Things like wet wipes, sheet masks, and blotting sheets are only used once before being trashed. Ninety-three percent of sewer blockages in the U.K. came from wet wipes made by combining fabric and plastic (Rai, 2019).

Junk Clothing: "Fast" Fashion's High Waste Footprint

Is your closet stuffed with clothing you've never worn? Perhaps some of it still has price tags attached. Or maybe you've worn an item just two or three times, only to have it tear in a place where it's impossible to repair? Do you find yourself sending clothing to a landfill because it's poor quality—or just to make room in your closet for more? If you answered "yes" to these questions, you might have been sucked into the "fast fashion" trend.

What is "Fast Fashion?"

This is the speedy production of the latest catwalk fashion replicas, enabling shops to rapidly sell large quantities of cheap, mass-produced clothes that reflect fleeting style trends. In fact, leading brands now release an astounding 52 collections a year (Marsh, 2022). Retailers receive a wider variety of cheap goods, which they are able to turn around quickly.

The term was first used in the early 1990s, when label Zara told the media that they intended to move garments from the design stage to being available in stores within just 15 days (Maiti, 2020). While consumers love it, this rapid turnaround came with a slew of consequences for nature, besides encouraging massive amounts of waste (as much as 85% of all textiles produced—3 out of every 5 fast fashion garments produced—are sent to landfills each year.) (Maiti, 2020; Marsh, 2022). This is not surprising when you consider that global consumers buy a staggering 80 billion new clothing items every year. This represents a 400% increase in consumption within the last two decades (Maiti, 2020).

Clothing production is the second-most water-intensive industry in the world, using almost 2 trillion cubic feet of water every year. Cotton, a sought-after natural fiber, is particularly problematic in this respect. Irrigating the amount of cotton required to produce a pair of jeans uses 1,800 gallons of water, while a cotton shirt requires 700 gallons (Maiti, 2020). Coloring clothes also uses vast quantities of freshwater and chemical dyes. The wastewater is usually returned untreated to local waterways, contaminating freshwater supplies for thousands of people.

Leather tanneries in Bangladesh are a good example. Despite being a big employer and economic contributor, the industry is unregulated, and tanneries release around 22,000 cubic meters of toxic wastewater into nearby rivers every day (Marsh, 2022). Chemicals and minerals like chromium, sulfur, and manganese now pollute local water sources. Almost 20,000 people are experiencing health issues ranging from skin rashes to respiratory diseases linked to this pollution. In 2010, 3 workers died after inhaling chemicals in tanneries (Marsh, 2022).

As previously mentioned in this book, producers are further able to cut costs by using synthetic textiles made from plastic or its derivatives. Washing these clothes releases around half a million tons of microfibers into the ocean annually; in 2017, the International Union for the Conservation of Nature (IUCN) estimated that as much as thirty-five percent of all microplastics in the oceans came from laundering synthetic fabrics (Maiti, 2020).

Most manufacturers rely on fossil fuels to power their factories, which release greenhouse gasses like carbon dioxide into the atmosphere. This is driving global warming, which in turn is leading to climate change. If you buy fast fashion, you are indirectly contributing to this, as clothing production emits around 10% of global carbon emissions—as much as the entire European Union (Maiti, 2020).

Tech and Electronics: Our Toxic Addiction to Gadgets

Once, there were no mobile phones. Computers took up entire rooms, and had to be moved with special trucks. The internet was used mainly by the military. You had to wait for mail to reach you, and for people to call you back from fixed line phones—if they got the message or remembered to switch on their answering machines!

Today's smartphones are no longer just communications devices; they're tiny personal computers. Apps deliver copious amounts of information, from weather reports and online games to helping us identify constellations, birds, and butterflies. Our phones have become like umbilical cords connecting us to the entire world, making these devices difficult to ignore.

Internet Addiction

There's a new anxiety syndrome affecting around 73% of people: misplacing their phones (Haynes, 2018). In addition, excessive smartphone use can cause increased anxiety and depression, poor sleep quality, and higher risks of injury and death in vehicle accidents. So why are we addicted to tech?

Dopamine, a "feel good" chemical in our brains, is released when we have enjoyable experiences, including successful social interactions. Certain "reward pathways" release dopamine in the brain, heightening the association between a particular stimulus or behavior, and the subsequent feel-good reward. The more this happens, the stronger the association becomes. In a sense, the brain becomes "trained" to respond with pleasure to a repetitive stimulus. Our phones, and especially social media, supply hundreds of opportunities for us to have pleasurable experiences through "likes," "clicks," messages, pictures, and other actions that elicit a dopamine surge in our brains.

And, if you're wondering, there really *is* such a thing as internet addiction, a disorder that affects 8–38% of Americans and Europeans (Gregory, 2016). It's a hard habit to break, as the internet and its byproducts are integral to our everyday lives.

As if that's not enough, our dependence on digital technologies is wreaking havoc on natural systems.

Mining

Smartphones and devices contain numerous minerals to keep them functioning, like copper, tellurium (which strengthens metals), lithium, cobalt, manganese, and tungsten. Then there are "rare earth" elements (REEs)—essential components of digital goods that make hard drives, screens, and batteries function properly. These elements are found in low concentrations in minerals and are hard to separate from other elements. Demand is spiking, mainly due to the boom in renewable energy alternatives, and could increase six-fold by 2040 (Nayar, 2021).

REEs are mined by putting the ore into leaching ponds, which leak if not properly lined, releasing their toxic chemicals into waterways and groundwater. Rare earth mining releases 2,000 tons of toxic waste for every ton of REEs produced, including 28 pounds of dust, 33,900–42,377 cubic feet of waste gas, 2,648 cubic feet of wastewater, and one ton of radioactive residue (Nayar, 2021).

China produces around 85% of REEs, followed by Australia at 10%. China is also looking to expand into Africa and the U.S. (the latter produces around 15,000 tons of REEs annually) (Nayar, 2021).

Manufacturing

Digital component parts need repeated treatment and cleaning during production, which uses a surprising amount of water. The average semiconductor chip factory alone uses between two and four gallons of water per day (Poor, 2019). Because cleaning requires the use of toxic solvents, this water becomes contaminated with heavy metals and other harmful elements, which can negatively impact local water supplies.

Transport

Digital goods need to be transported from the places where they were produced to consumers, sometimes in other countries. While ocean freighters are used—and are generally more efficient than other transportation options—they run on low-grade fuel oil that contains as much as 35,000 parts per million of sulfur. This is one of the reasons why maritime shipping accounts for as much as 8% of global sulfur dioxide emissions, as well as significant emissions of particulate matter (Wang, 2014).

Energy Use

Digital technologies need electricity—a resource that's mainly produced by fossil fuels (coal, oil, and natural gas) worldwide. Electricity is used both during manufacturing and when devices are used. In 2012, digital technology networks used around 5% of global electricity, which is set to increase to 20% by 2025 (ICT Works, 2020). However, most of these devices generate a considerable amount of heat, which is indicative of their inefficiency, and air conditioning for cooling is rarely factored into electricity use. Digital technologies like Bitcoin also use considerable amounts of energy: In 2020, it was consuming 73.12 terawatt hours of electricity, the same as the whole of Australia, and produced just under 11 kilotons of e-waste (ICT Works 2020).

Ethereum, the network behind the second-largest cryptocurrency after Bitcoin, will soon be changing the type of blockchain mechanism they use in a process known as "the merge." This, they say, will make Ethereum at least 99% more energy efficient than Bitcoin (IANS, 2022).

Tech's High Carbon Footprint

It is believed that the digital technology and communications sector may be responsible for as much as 1.8–3.9% of global carbon emissions, which is likely to increase over time. This is more than the 2% the aviation industry generates (Rosane, 2021). Digital goods and electronics have carbon emissions built into the entire life cycle, from manufacturing to end use. Improvements in efficiency tend to elicit increased demand, thus negating energy savings. Switching to renewable energy sources is not necessarily an answer. The production of solar panels, wind turbines, and the like also creates emissions, and increases demand for rare metals, such as silver and certain REEs. Ideally, the industry should aim to become more sustainable, reducing the planned obsolescence built into its current business model.

Disposal and Waste

The technology sector generally embraces replacement rather than repairing old or outdated digital goods, spurred by innovation and the promise of a newer model with more capabilities. Mobile phones, for instance, are generally replaced every two years, while software upgrades often lead to hardware upgrades (ICT Works, 2020). Although this approach increases profits for manufacturers, it encourages redundancy, and is causing a monumental waste problem, as many digital goods are simply trashed when they become obsolete.

A great deal of the materials used in digital goods are not recovered but enter landfills as part of general waste. In 2014, about a ton of electronic waste (e-waste) was produced. By 2019, this had escalated to around 50 million tons, only 20% of which was being properly disposed of (ICT Works, 2020).

Few of the materials used in digital products biodegrade, and many corrode. They may release heavy metals and toxins as they weather, which eventually find their way into water supplies. While recycling exists, the practicalities tend to be complex.

Some manufacturers solve the problem by shipping their waste to developing countries with lax environmental regulations.

Having read this chapter, you are probably feeling a little despairing when you consider the environmental impact of your lifestyle. The good news is that there are a number of swaps and hacks that you can do to live lighter on this planet.

Chapter 3:

Everyday Eco-habits: Swaps and Tricks

If you've ever taken a walk along a beach close to human habitation, a city street, or a suburban stream, you will likely have been confronted with plastic trash, mainly in the form of single-use bottles. You will probably see other discarded plastics as well: food wrappers, drinking straws, and bits of packaging. An internet search will throw up images of once-pristine beaches and rivers choked with plastic that has been thrown "away." The truth is, on Earth, there is no "away;" trash simply ends up somewhere else, whether in a landfill, a public park, or perhaps that beach you like to visit on your annual vacations.

One of the main components of this particular waste stream are single-use items, such as water or soft drink bottles, straws, food wrappers, takeout containers, plastic cutlery, and packaging.

How Did We Get Here?

Nearly every piece of plastic ever produced still exists in some form, somewhere, and it has spawned a significant waste stream.

A stupendous 10 million tons of plastic ends up in our oceans every year (Plastic Oceans International, 2018). And if you think that doesn't affect you, think again. One hundred percent of all mussels tested contain microplastics (plastics that have broken down into microscopic particles), and humans are believed to consume over forty pounds of plastic in their lifetime (Plastic Oceans International, 2018). Ninety-one percent of plastic is also not recycled, and ends up in landfills and natural environments everywhere (EDN Staff, 2022).

In landfills, plastic breaks down to smaller and smaller particles. These are toxic, and contaminate soils and waterways. They are often ingested by birds and animals mistaking plastic particles for food, which has a detrimental effect on the organism. I am sure we've all read the media reports of creatures dying of starvation because their stomachs are full of plastic. Although ocean microplastic pollution has received a great deal of press coverage, researchers in Germany established that plastic pollution on land is actually 4–23 times higher, depending on the location of the pollution (EDN Staff, 2022). Having so much plastic contaminating natural systems could ultimately be detrimental to both human and animal health.

Despite the hype around becoming a "paperless" society, we all use and waste considerable amounts of paper. In 2009, paper trash accounted for 26 million metric tons (or 16% of landfill solid waste). That means that around 1 billion trees-worth of paper are thrown away every year in the U.S., with commercial and industrial waste paper accounting for more than 40% of paper going to landfill (Gifford, 2014). Recycling can help. Recycling a ton of paper saves 17 mature trees, 7,000 gallons of water, 380 gallons of oil, 4,100 kilowatt hours of electricity, and 33 cubic yards of landfill space (Gifford, 2014). However, recycling alone won't save the planet. We need to reduce our paper use altogether.

While the focus on waste in the beauty industry tends to focus on over-packaging, there is another aspect: wasting the products themselves. Retailers send unsold inventory and expired products back to producers, while unused—or partly used—products take up shelf space in your home. Some industry executives believe that as much as 20–40% of beauty products are ultimately wasted (Cernansky, 2021).

What Can You Do? Environmental Swaps and Hacks at Home

The best way to reduce waste at home—and save natural environments, resources, and raw materials—is not to generate it in the first place. When you think about it consciously, there are plenty of ways to use less plastic and paper, buy less cosmetics, avoid fast fashion, and use digital and electronic goods for longer.

Toward Waste-Free Takeout

Takeout is notorious for coming packaged with side servings of plastic, as well as mixed-materials packaging that is almost impossible to recycle. Here are a few tips as to how to be prepared to avoid the unsustainable trash trap when ordering takeout:

- Swap plastic cutlery for home cutlery. When ordering, ask the restaurant to leave out the plastic cutlery, paper napkins, sauce sachets, and any other single-use items. Plastic cutlery is usually made from polystyrene (which is also used to make styrofoam), and is almost impossible to recycle. Carry your own cutlery kit in your purse or car, to use when you're traveling, or if you're ordering takeout on the run.

- Speaking of which, opt for a reusable coffee cup rather than single-use cups. Take your own thermos or reusable coffee cup when ordering takeout coffee—or, better yet, drink the beverage at the coffee shop, from a ceramic cup. Disposable coffee cups cannot be recycled because of the wax coating, which is usually made of plastic resin. The colored lids might look trendy, but they're made of plastic too.

- Another single-use plastic item is drinking straws. In the U.S., around 500 million straws are thrown away every day, which works out to around 180 billion a year. Extrapolate that further, and that's just over 3 million pounds of plastic sent to landfills or entering the ocean daily (Hutchings, 2018). Swap your plastic drinking straw for a reusable one made from stainless steel or bamboo.

- Some restaurants that deliver food to customers are already ahead of the game. UberEats, Postmates, and GrubHub for example now require customers to specifically request single-use items like plastic cutlery and straws (Postmates, after joining the campaign in 2019, estimated that it had saved 122 million packets of plastic cutlery from entering the waste stream.) (Arria-Devoe, n.d.).

- DeliverZero, based in New York City, is an online platform enabling customers to order food from restaurants that deliver in reusable containers.

Reduce Your Shopping Footprint

- Five trillion plastic bags are produced globally every year. Not only are they made using non-renewable fossil fuels like oil, they take up to 1,000 years to decompose. And, while they do, they entangle wildlife and birds, and end up being eaten by sea creatures that mistake floating bags for jellyfish and other food. Americans alone throw away some 1oo billion bags annually—that's about 307 bags per person (EDN Staff, 2022). To avoid contributing to this waste stream, opt for reusable shopping bags instead of mindlessly buying plastic ones at the store when you do your grocery shopping. If you forget your reusable tote at home, ask the store for paper bags, or even a cardboard box that can be recycled or put into your compost heap, if you have one. It's a good idea to carry reusable bags in your purse or the trunk of your vehicle so you don't forget them at home.

- Packaging constituted the biggest demand for plastic packaging in 2017, accounting for nearly 161 tons (EDN Staff, 2022). Instead of buying packaged products, buy more food items in bulk or loose, taking your own jars or net bags to the store. This is a very easy and economical swap, as it's usually cheaper to buy items in bulk. Packed foods not only contain unhealthy preservatives and chemicals, they often cost more. Buy larger sizes if you don't have a bulk store in your area, so that you don't need to shop as frequently.

In the next section, we'll consider each room in your home, and explain how you can get started with easy swaps and hacks to reduce your waste stream and planetary footprint.

Waste-Free Home

Kitchen

It's essential that we wean ourselves off single-use plastic, especially bottles. Instead of using single-use bottles, invest in a stainless steel water bottle. Many of these keep cold beverages chilled and warm beverages hot, so are more beneficial than regular storage containers.

Instead of wrapping leftovers or covering bowls with plastic wrap or aluminum, use reusable food wraps made of cotton coated in plant-based waxes, tree resins, or beeswax. Use them as you would cling wrap over bowls and plates, or to wrap sandwiches, vegetables, and fruit. The warmth from your hands softens the wraps enough to stick. They're easy to clean: Simply wipe them down with a dishcloth and some diluted dish soap, and store for reuse.

Use cloth napkins instead of paper ones. You can get creative by using a different color for different family members, or choosing elegant fabric designs.

Use cloth rags rather than paper towels. You can also cut up old clothing for rags.

Use Swedish dishcloths or similar brands. These contain 70% cellulose and 30% cotton, they're durable, and reusable. They absorb 20 times their weight in water, work as well as paper towels, and dry quickly with no odors (Thompson, 2021).

Avoid using paper or styrofoam cups and plates but opt for more durable, washable ones instead. Purchase them from the thrift store to use for picnics and barbecues. You can also ask guests to bring their own. If you must use paper products, try to buy ones with recycled content. You can also buy paper plates and cups made from more environmentally-friendly materials such as bamboo, cornstarch, sugarcane waste (or bagasse), or even hemp.

Opt for reusable coffee filters made from metal mesh or unbleached cloth instead of paper ones. Some of the chlorine and dioxins used when bleaching the paper can also end up in your coffee. And who wants that?

Replace single-use tea bags with a tea ball or tea strainer, and start using loose leaf tea. Paper tea bags contain several toxins, pesticides, and dioxins, so you shouldn't be drinking tea stored in them anyway. Many tea bags are also bleached with chlorine, and made of materials that don't break down in the environment (some are even made of plastic.). Opt for loose leaf tea—and your body will thank you for it.

Store dry goods in mason or tin jars instead of using plastic containers. You can also pack things like homemade soup, parfaits, preserves, and other foods. You can even drink smoothies, coffee, and water from mason jars.

Nonstick or Teflon cookware is usually plastic coated, so consider stainless steel, ceramic, or cast iron alternatives.

Bathroom

Bathrooms harbor a surprising amount of plastic. As much as 50% of bathroom products are not recycled, adding 552 million plastic bottles to landfills every year (McCoy, 2021). In 2018, the U.S. cosmetics and personal care industry alone used 7.9 billion units of rigid plastic (Plastic Pollution Coalition, 2022).

Add a recycle bin to your bathroom and become aware of just how much plastic and other waste your beauty and personal care routines actually generate. Find and support no-waste brands and options wherever possible.

Here are several bathroom swaps and hacks to get you started.

- Every time you have an option to buy things packaged in glass instead of plastic, do so. Glass is better for the environment than plastic, and is fully recyclable, as is metal or steel packaging.
- Use toilet paper made from recycled paper. Four hundred and thirty four thousand trees would be saved if every U.S. household replaced just one virgin toilet roll with one made of recycled paper (Gifford, 2014).

Alternatively, you can use family cloth or washable cloth wipes—or install a bidet in your bathroom.

- Use bar soap in the shower and for hand washing instead of pump or liquid soaps and body washes that come with lots of plastic packaging that is often not recyclable. Bar soaps can even be purchased without wrappers. You can also buy shampoo and conditioner bars for washing your hair.

- As far as dental care goes, swap your plastic toothbrush for a bamboo one. Ditch the mouthwash bottle by using mouthwash tablets, which dissolve in water. Switch from nylon to plastic-free silk or charcoal floss, preferably in plastic-free or recyclable packaging. And look for toothpaste in an aluminum tube rather than a plastic one.

- Swap Q-Tips for reusable ear swabs.

- Switch to a safety razor rather than using a disposable plastic one.

- When it's that time of the month, use period pants or a menstrual cup instead of tampons and sanitary napkins, both of which contain plastic. It'll save you money, too.

- When it comes to your beauty routine, make sure that you finish a particular product before buying another. Start off by reducing the number of products you use, and reuse the containers wherever possible. You can also recycle any glass, metal, cardboard, or paper packaging. Look for products packaged in containers marked with recycling symbols #1 and #2, as these are recyclable. Alternatively, send your packaging waste to TerraCycle, which allows you to ship your used cosmetic packaging to them for recycling.

- Look for biodegradable products and waterless formulas, which require simpler packaging that is smaller and lighter. One sustainable beauty brand specializing in such products is Unwrapped Life.

- Another option is to consider brands that create personalized skin and hair care products tailored to your needs, such as Pure Culture. UpCircle Beauty makes products derived from food waste like mandarin oranges and used coffee grounds.

- Make your own personal care products and cosmetics. You can also make your own facial and body scrubs, and facemasks. Try using used coffee grounds as an exfoliant for softer skin rather than commercial beauty products.

- Skip the makeup remover and use natural oils, such as olive, jojoba, or coconut oil instead, depending on your skin type.

- Use a sustainable mud mask rather than a single-use sheet mask. Companies such as Credo Beauty have replaced many single-use items, including sheet masks and makeup remover wipes with more sustainable options.

- Replace cotton balls, that often come in plastic bags, with reusable cotton cloths.

Bedroom and Living Room

- Banish clothing containing synthetic fabrics, such as nylon, polyester, and rayon (or viscose) from your wardrobe. The reason? An astonishing 60% of all clothing today contains plastic, with about 63% of these "fabrics" deriving from virgin plastics. In the U.S. alone, around 10.2 million tons of clothing derived from plastic is produced annually (Melina, 2022). Switching to regular cotton is not necessarily the answer either, as it takes thousands of gallons of water to grow and produce, not to mention synthetic fertilizers and toxic pesticides. Rather, buy less clothing, and wash it less frequently. Swap synthetics for organic cotton, linen, hemp or bamboo.

- When washing these items, use a laundry bag designed to catch the microfibers before they enter your wastewater system. Guppyfriend and Cora Ball are two popular options.

- Tailor clothes that no longer fit, or alter old clothing to create a new look. Add ribbons, buttons, lace trimming, or new closures. Turn jeans into shorts, or cut up old clothing for quilts and other sewing projects.

- The same goes for items like bed linen, floor rugs, drapes, pillows, cushions, and other soft furnishings in the home: Many of these are also made from plastic fabrics. Rather opt for natural fabrics. Instead of fabric drapes, consider blinds made of natural materials such as bamboo. Or make your own blinds if you're handy with needles and thread.

- Choose wooden coat hangers instead of plastic ones.

- If you like candles, choose ones in glass jars that you can refill.

- Decorate with plants to bring the outdoors in. Some pot plants even purify the air.

Study (or Home-Office)

- Use a whiteboard or the Notes app on your phone for grocery lists, reminders, and announcements.

- Change your bills to "paperless," and pay them online or with mobile banking.

- One hundred million trees are felled each year for junk mail alone. Refuse it wherever possible. Click the "No" option on forms requesting permission for companies, stores, and outlets to send you advertising material, specials or other forms of junk mail. There are a number of apps that assist with removing your name from mailing lists as well.

- Use both sides of paper sheets or reuse printed paper for notes, sketches, packaging filler, etc.

- Opt for online subscriptions rather than printed ones for magazines, newspapers, newsletters, circulars, and the like.

- Invest in an ereader for subscriptions, as well as digital books. You can also purchase audio books, which you can listen to while you do chores, work in the garden, exercise, or drive.

- Buy recycled paper as much as possible.

- Don't mindlessly click the "print" button. Think before you print, and print only what is necessary. Only print the relevant pages of a document. Print on both sides of the paper, and adjust the size so that you use less paper.

- Use cloud software when working collaboratively on projects rather than hard copies. Distribute files using Dropbox, Google Docs, or WeTransfer.

- Share digital files with colleagues and friends using flash drives rather than printed copies of documents.

If you've started implementing these eco-hacks and swaps, you might want to go all out and adopt a zero waste household altogether. In the next chapter, I'll explain how you can achieve this.

Finally, if you are enjoying reading this book and are finding it helpful, remember to leave a review. As an independent author with a small marketing budget, reviews are my livelihood on this platform. I love hearing from my readers and I personally read every single review.

Chapter 4:
Achieving a Zero Waste Household

In 2014, U.S. photographer Gregg Segal, who told *Smithsonian* magazine that he had always been fascinated and somewhat perturbed by garbage, decided to photograph people posing with a week's worth of the trash they had accumulated. Afterward, some of his subjects became more aware of their consumption habits and waste production, while others simply felt overwhelmed. I guess that would apply to many of us, who happily toss trash into the garbage can without really thinking about the implications. But there *is* a way for individuals and households to curb and reduce their personal waste streams.

The Zero Waste Lifestyle: An Introduction

The zero waste movement encourages individuals to reduce the amount of trash they throw away every day, ultimately aiming to send as little as possible to landfills. While it is very difficult to produce virtually no waste, there are many ways to reduce the consumption that generates garbage in the first place. People involved in zero waste, reuse and recycle as much as possible, and avoid purchasing single-use items.

Adopting this lifestyle can be challenging at first, as newbies need to change sometimes years of wasteful behavior, becoming much more aware of their consumption habits. Some people belong to zero waste online communities, who offer support and encouragement, hints, and tips. The process usually begins with making small changes: establishing a compost heap in the garden, repurposing items instead of buying new, avoiding single-use purchases, and recycling. It may take a long time to become entirely zero waste, if ever. While there are those who have reduced their household trash to just a pint-sized jar a year, most people simply aim to get as close to zero as possible.

The idea behind the movement is that, if you refuse to buy or accept products with wasteful packaging, demand will decline, and manufacturers will be forced to reconsider their options, as is happening in the cosmetics industry. Refusing to purchase single-use plastic will not only eliminate toxins from your life and the environment, you will also be doing something to reduce humanity's plastic consumption. Downsizing your shopping list will simplify your life, giving you more time to spend on things that really matter to you.

Adopting a zero waste lifestyle has many positive effects: It reduces our environmental footprint, relieves pressure on natural systems, promotes biodiversity, and encourages sustainable living.

Getting Started

One of the first—and best—places to get started is to take a good look at your trash. This isn't the most appealing thing to do but it's probably the best way to evaluate your lifestyle, and the extent to which you throw things away or send them to landfills. What forms the bulk of your trash? Is it single-use plastic?; Compostable food waste, like vegetable peelings or coffee grounds?; Is it disposable items, like diapers, razors, sheet masks, or ear buds?; What portion of your trash consists of packaging?

This will give you a very good idea of where your starting point should be. If you're a lodestone for single-use plastic, take a look at the previous chapter for ideas as to how to swap single-use items for more durable ones. Start a compost heap in your garden as a first step to reusing your food waste (your plants will love you for it too). Invest in more durable items if your trash consists of disposables: hankies, straight razors, mud face masks, and cloth diapers—to name just a few. If there's a disproportionate amount of packaging in your trash, consider buying in bulk and taking your own reusable jars and containers to the store. Alter your shopping habits to reduce the amount of waste your household produces. Switch to brands that use simpler packaging, and lobby manufacturers to use less—or offer recyclable options.

The Zero Waste Pyramid

Zero waste can be summed up by what's popularly termed the "zero waste pyramid." Originally developed by Bea Johnson, who also introduced the trash jar that epitomizes the zero waste lifestyle, this inverted pyramid provides guidance as to how to deal with situations where waste can potentially be generated. It's especially helpful if you're a beginner. The U.S. Environmental Protection Agency has also developed one.

However, I have altered Bea's standard waste pyramid to include repair, as I believe this is an important aspect of achieving a zero waste lifestyle (I will go into more detail on this shortly.)

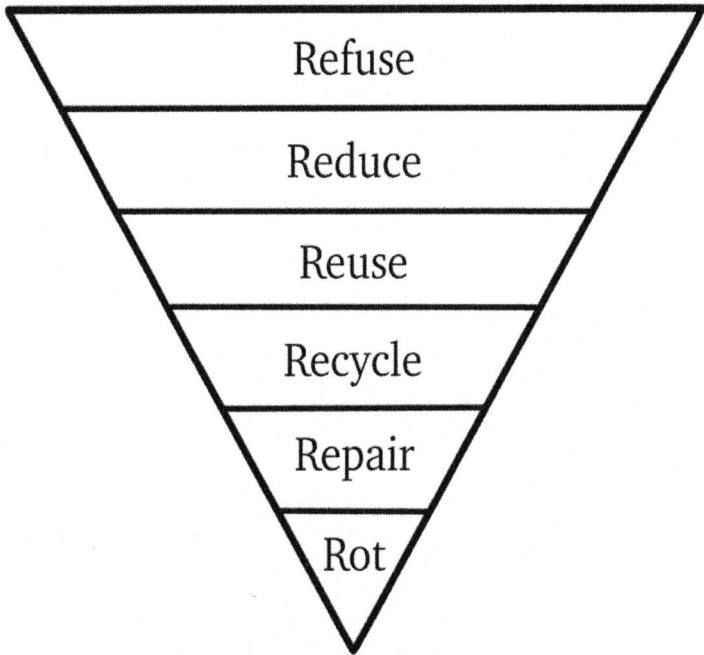

Refuse

Reduce

Reuse

Recycle

Repair

Rot

I would encourage you, the reader, to draw this graphic on a scrap of paper, and put it up in an area of your home where it's most likely to help you to keep sustainability in mind:

- Firstly, **refuse** to buy what you don't need, which prevents unwanted items from entering your home in the first place. Everyone's situation is different, but this could include promotional items, single-use plastic, and junk mail. This is by far the best way of saving resources and reducing your waste stream.

- Next, **reduce** what you use. Think about this for a minute. We all have items that we use wastefully.

- It's also important to **reuse** what you can. Extend the life of items by mending, handing down, and repairing them. Consider buying secondhand items rather than new ones, or sell things you no longer use or need. Reusing also means swapping disposable items for reusable ones.

- Start **recycling**. At this point, it's worth pointing out that recycling is not always the panacea that it's purported to be. Many things never make it to the recycle bin, or are assigned to landfill anyway because they contain a mixture of materials that are hard to separate. Recycling is also not a final solution, as recycled items may eventually end up in landfill once they have been recycled a certain amount of times. It's better to reduce your purchasing as a first resort.

- Another type of recycling, usually referred to as **upcycling**, is the process of turning materials that would otherwise be discarded into new products, often of higher value and with a greater environmental purpose. Reusing something designed for one purpose for something else can also be a form of upcycling. You can do this at home. Consider turning old T-shirts into facemasks or reusable produce bags. Old soda bottles can be cut in half to make self-watering pots for kitchen herbs or other plants. Cut and hem old fabric to make reusable cotton rounds to use for removing makeup, staunching wounds, and other uses. Larger pieces of fabric can be used for unusual and reusable gift wrap— you might start a trend among your friends and relatives! Turn candy jars or the glass jars that once contained candles into storage containers for paper clips, elastic bands, and other small items. Turn old dresser drawers into a garden feature by using them as an unusual planter. Add a handle to old tin cans, paint them, and use them as bird feeders, watering cans, planters, or cutlery holders—the list is endless.

- **Repairing** faulty or damaged items was once a way of life, but this principle has disappeared in recent decades. When we repair broken or faulty stuff, it can be used once more. This can apply to anything, from broken furniture to electrical appliances that no longer function as they should. Fixing things is very sustainable and definitely saves on both natural and manufactured resources, carbon emissions, your budget, and landfill space.

- What happens to the rest? **Rot** or **compost** whatever doesn't fit into the above categories. Examples of compostable items include some types of food scraps, waste paper, and wooden or bamboo toothbrushes. This returns nutrients to the soil.

Tips From a Zero Waste Expert

So how do you practically implement the principles encapsulated in the zero waste pyramid at home? Here are some of Bea Johnson's tips:

- Eliminate surfaces in your home, as these tend to attract wasteful clutter.

- Buy secondhand items for your closet and stick to the basics. You can work with as little as 15 mix-and-match items.

- Make your own cosmetics and personal care products to avoid having to worry about excess packaging or toxic ingredients.

- Opt for a minimalistic approach to home decor—no clutter, no mess, just the basics.

- When shopping, focus on items you can buy loose to ditch the packaging and save on your grocery budget.

- Avoid fresh produce pre-packed in plastic.

- Make your own cloth bags from old sheets or clothing, and use these for dry goods when shopping at bulk stores. Use old crayons to write on the bags, so you know what's in them.

- When buying meat or fish, head to the counter and ask for items to fill your reusable containers with rather than buying packaged foods off the shelves.

- Store dry goods in reusable glass jars when you get home.

- Compost kitchen waste such as vegetable peelings.

- Forget about paper towels: use a washcloth instead.

- Use the minimum of household cleaners—you can do a lot with liquid soap and vinegar (see recipes and ideas below.)

Recipes for Homemade Household Cleaners

Bathroom Cleaner

This will work for both the tub and shower, as well as on the tile floors. Fill a jar with 1 ½ cups of baking soda, ½ cup of warm water, ½ cup of liquid soap, and 2 tablespoons of white distilled vinegar. If your grout is really grimy, add a touch of lemon juice (Earley, 2021).

All-Purpose Cleaning Spray With Vinegar

This will clean just about anything, from countertops to light fixtures. It's really easy to make. Mix 13 ounces of hot water with ½ cup of white vinegar, 15 drops of grapefruit essential oil, 10 drops of lavender essential oil, and 7 drops of lemon essential oil in a spray bottle (Earley, 2021).

DIY All-Purpose Cleaning Spray Without Vinegar

Acidic homemade cleaner ingredients like lemon and vinegar have some drawbacks: They can leave dull spots on soft surfaces like marble, and erode the sealant on granite counters, for example. To counteract this, use a gentler but equally effective cleaner. Mix together ¼ cup of vodka, 2 ¾ cups of distilled water (regular tap water may cause streaking), ¼ teaspoon of lavender essential oil, and ⅛ of a teaspoon of tea tree essential oil (Early, 2021). Pour the mixture into a spray bottle, and you're all set to clean.

Window and Glass Cleaner

To achieve a streak-free window clean, use cornstarch. That's right. Combine 1 cup of hot water and 1 cup of rubbing alcohol in a large bowl. Then whisk in 4 tablespoons of cornstarch (Earley, 2021). Transfer the mixture into a spray bottle. To use, simply spritz onto windows, mirrors, or any other glass, and wipe it clean with a microfiber cloth.

Hardwood Floor Cleaner

Dish soap makes an ideal cleaner for hardwood floors (who would have guessed?). Mix 2 tablespoons of dish soap with a gallon of warm water, and mop the floors (Earley, 2021).

The internet is a great resource for plenty of homemade cleaner recipes. Search for ones with simple, affordable ingredients that are easy to come by, and your home can sparkle without the addition of harmful, unsustainable chemicals and ingredients.

Recycling Realities

Many years ago, a friend of mine was an environmental education officer, and one of the topics they used to teach scholars was the three Rs—reduce, reuse, and recycle. The guides would empty a bag of trash on the grass and the scholars would need to decide what could be reused or recycled. Then the group would talk about ways to reduce their trash. If they were lucky, there would be a thinker in the group: "Shouldn't we just buy less stuff?"

Recycling presents a conundrum. On the one hand, it is a valid way of reusing resources, but on the other, it makes us complacent about our waste and the planetary footprint of our consumption. This means that we aren't as informed about recycling as we should be, with many people simply assuming that everything they throw away is recyclable. This is called "hopecycling" when all trash goes into the recycle bin in the hopes that it will be reused. The trouble is, that when it reaches the recycling center, most of the load turns out not to be recyclable. It's usually too time consuming and expensive to sift out the recyclables, so the whole lot goes to landfill anyway. So don't hopecycle. If you're going to recycle, do it properly.

Recycling Symbols: Everything You Need to Know

Most of us are familiar with the recycling symbol: arrows arranged in a triangle. When you buy a plastic item, or something packaged in a plastic container, you've probably noticed that there's a number in the middle of the symbol. These numbers are an essential guide as to what type of plastic is in the product or packaging, and whether it can be recycled or not.

It's worth noting that different cities and towns accept different types of plastic for recycling, so it's best to contact your local recycling center or municipality to find out which plastic recycle numbers can and cannot be recycled by them. Some may also have special rules about certain types of containers. For example, in Baltimore, Maryland, all seven types of plastics are accepted in their curbside recycling program. However, they specifically prohibit plastic bags, clam shell containers, antifreeze and motor oil containers, foam, wax-coated paper items, paper towels and napkins, the greasy half of pizza boxes, shredded paper, and pesticide and spray paint cans.

Here's a breakdown of what those recycle numbers mean.

No 1: Polyethylene Terephthalate (PETE/PET)

PET is a lightweight plastic that's easy to recycle, and it's in fact the most frequently recycled plastic type. It's used for many single-use bottles, including those that contain soft drinks, peanut butter, salad dressing, mineral water, fruit juice, and even cooking oil. It's accepted by most curbside recycling programs.

No. 2: High-Density Polyethylene (HDPE)

Most curbside programs also accept this type of plastic, as it can be recycled into a variety of items, from flower pots to trash cans. HDPE is used for packaging milk, household cleaners, laundry detergent, shampoo, butter, motor oil, and fruit juice.

No. 3: Polyvinyl Chloride (PVC)

This type of plastic is found in shower curtains, piping, clear food packaging, and cooking oil bottles, as well as a wide variety of other items. While some plastic lumber makers will accept it, it's one of the least recycled plastic types due to additives. As technology improves, recycling centers are slowly able to accept items they couldn't before, but PVC is not one of these.

No. 4: Low-Density Polyethylene (LDPE)

LDPE is used to make plastic wrap, grocery bags, bread bags, and frozen food bags. Check with your local recycle center to see if this type of plastic is accepted.

No. 5: Polypropylene (PP)

This type of plastic is used to make yogurt containers, margarine containers, syringes, bottle caps, and straws (which is another reason to refuse the straw with your drink.). It can be recycled into plastic lumber, car battery cases, garbage cans, and brooms.

No. 6: Polystyrene (PS)

Also known as styrofoam, this material is used for both protective packaging and packing peanuts, disposable beverage cups, takeout food containers, meat trays, and egg cartons. Find out whether your local municipality accepts PS for recycling, as some areas do. It can be recycled into egg cartons, foam packaging, and insulation.

No. 7: Other

This is a miscellaneous category for all other types of plastic, like resins, acrylic, and nylon. The most common types of No. 7

plastic are headlight lenses, sport and baby bottles, sippy cups, and safety shields. This mixed resin category is the most difficult type of plastic to recycle. Polycarbonate leaches bisphenol A (BPA), a known endocrine disruptor.

Surprising Recyclable Items

Some of the items that can be recycled, apart from plastic, will surprise you. Here's a list of some unusual recyclables:

- Pet fur is used to make the booms placed in the ocean during oil spills to protect the shoreline. Pet fur can be sent to Matter of Trust for recycling.

- Batteries are a landfill hazard, as they leak acid when they decompose. In some states, it's actually illegal to send batteries containing nickel, cadmium or lead to landfills. However, Call2Recycle is the biggest battery recycling program in the U.S., and they'll gladly take used batteries off your hands. They also have drop-off locations throughout the States, including Lowe's Home Improvement stores.

- Both Home Depot and Lowe's stores will take your used fluorescent bulbs and recycle them for free.

- If you're an avid gardener, you'll probably have accumulated several plastic pots or old seedling trays in your garage or garden shed. If your local municipality doesn't accept them for recycling, Home Depot and Lowe's stores will.

- If your favorite pair of Nike sneakers has finally given up on you, take them back to Nike! That may sound strange, but the company takes back their old sneakers and melts them down to produce new ones. Unfortunately, they'll only take Nikes. However, North Face will take any sneaker brand, and will also give you a discount coupon toward your next purchase up to a certain value. Many local running stores also collect shoes, sometimes giving you a discount when you donate them.

- Well-loved jeans can be hard to part with, which is why so many of us cut them down into cut-off shorts, or use them for rags or quilting. However, manufacturer Madewell will take any brand of jeans, which they recycle into housing insulation. They'll also give you a discount voucher for your trouble.

- When you buy electronic goods, ask the store what their buy-back policy is. Some stores will take back old electronics for free. Some may even offer credits toward a purchase at their stores.

- Billions of used contact lenses are flushed every year—and end up in our oceans. But did you know that if you're a contact wearer, you can take your old lenses to Bausch and Lomb? They'll even accept the blister packs they're packaged in, and will pay for the shipping. What's not to like?

- Wondering what to do with that old carpet you replaced? Carpet America Recovery Effort turns old carpets into fibers or plastic pellets that can be used to make new carpets.

- If your children have outgrown crayons, or you've ended up with small bits and pieces, you might be interested to know that The Crayon Initiative in California takes crayon donations. They melt them down and make new ones, which are donated to children's homes across the U.S.

- The age of CDs and DVDs is largely over, and many of us have old discs lying around. Before tossing them, contact the CD Recycling Center of America. They repurpose old CDs, DVDs, and even Blu-Ray discs to create plastic used in car manufacture and building materials.

Replacing Plastic with Biodegradable Alternatives

On the face of it, this looks like a great idea. A design student based in Iceland came up with a great solution to single-use plastic water bottles. By mixing powdered agar (a substance made from red algae) with water, he was able to create a biodegradable bottle. It begins to decompose as soon as it's empty. Unfortunately, agar has a tendency to tear, which means it's not suitable for mass production—yet. Some manufacturers are also making bottles that can be scrunched down to almost nothing to take up less landfill space. But would consumers use these alternatives?

The surprising answer is: maybe not. Take polystyrene packing peanuts, for instance. They take a very long time to decompose, and can float around in waterways or landfills for years. Today, you can get biodegradable packing peanuts, made from natural, non-toxic ingredients like cornstarch and wheat. They dissolve in water, and can be added to compost piles. However, they tend to weigh more than traditional packing peanuts, which means that shipping costs are higher. Production is also more expensive and, with today's economic situation, most producers and consumers would rather cut costs than switch to a more eco-friendly option. Having said that, you can use recycled packing peanuts that are color coded to indicate where the material originated. Green peanuts are made from at least 70% recycled materials, so these might make a good alternative (Heritage Paper, 2016).

A Note About "Greenwashing"

We're bombarded with words like "natural," "organic," and "eco-friendly" on packaging and in advertisements. But these descriptors are now used so often as to be almost meaningless. Together with "green" logos, artwork, and photographs, some companies may also be using such wording to greenwash their public image.

If you've never heard of it, "greenwashing" occurs when a company's marketing messages don't reflect its actions. In such cases, a company will claim to be eco-friendly—and may in fact be doing a few token activities—but its operations as a whole are having a detrimental impact on the natural environment. In countries such as Sweden, greenwashing has become so prevalent that the government has had to pass laws prohibiting it.

Greenwashing actually arose as a result of the sustainability movement, with more people wishing to have a smaller planetary footprint. Naturally, companies saw an opportunity to market their products, and started looking for ways to exploit consumers' newfound interest in environmental issues. In some cases, however, companies have merely seen an economic opportunity, and have not backed up their claims with tangible proof that their products or operations have a smaller environmental impact than before.

Greenwashing has several negative effects. By literally paying lip service to environmental principles while continuing on a path that would cause further planetary destruction places the Earth, humans, and all other life forms in jeopardy.

It also makes the public suspicious, as no one knows whether the claims companies and businesses are making are true. This means that some of the companies genuinely doing good are reluctant to go public for fear of being falsely accused of greenwashing. This is known as "greenhushing."

Another aspect of greenwashing is "scopewashing"—when companies report on the extent of their emissions in a misleading way. For example, they may reveal the direct emissions from their factories, but ignore indirect emissions from energy use, transport, or the sourcing of raw materials.

As a consumer, it can be very difficult to detect whether a company or brand is greenwashing because the facts are often hidden. It can take hours of research to unveil the truth, and companies know this.

The first step in establishing whether a company is greenwashing or not, is to do your research. Use the internet, follow their social media pages, and read their sustainability reports, annual reports, and similar documents. If you're doing your research and something seems off, it may be time to withdraw your support for that company and its brands.

Don't be fooled by clever, eco-friendly branding. If the claims the company is making seem too good to be true, that's a red flag right there. Very often, they are! Do their claims have any solid, scientific basis?; Can you verify the information?; Does the company or its products have any reliable certification?

In the next chapter, you'll find out more about how consumerism works against our best efforts to live lighter on the planet.

Chapter 5:

How Consumerism Works Against Green Living

There's nothing quite like moving from a big city to the country to truly appreciate the subtle influence of consumerism on our lives. Friends of mine who have done this generally found that the inconvenience took some getting used to, mostly because they couldn't get what they wanted when they wanted it—or at all. Over time, however, these people adapted. If there was only one variety of apples at the store, that's what they bought. Sometimes, they had to make their own alternatives, or adapt their plans to work around what was available locally.

Subsequently, when visiting big cities, the incredible variety available at malls and stores startled them. There seemed to be endless yogurt flavors, umpteen cakes on the menu at coffee shops, numerous clothing and furniture stores, and takeout restaurants by the dozen. It was mind-boggling. Without realizing it, they had become used to a less consumptive lifestyle, where life was slower, people were genuine, and there were different opportunities. They could grow their own vegetables, go for long nature walks, and discover the joy of being self-sufficient.

Today, we're all being encouraged through an endless stream of advertisements and promotions to consume voraciously. As a result, it's anticipated that by 203o, there will be around 5.6 billion consumers on the planet. And, if they all live like Americans do, we'll need at least 5 Earths-worth of resources to sustain us (The World Counts, 2020).

What is Consumerism?

Consumerism is "an economic and social ideology that encourages the consumption or acquisition of goods or services in a never-ending cycle" (Scott, 2017). The Merriam-Webster dictionary defines it as "a preoccupation with, and an inclination toward the buying of consumer goods." The defining characteristic of consumption is that it often goes far beyond simply satisfying one's basic needs. Seducing consumers with the false promise that having more will automatically bring on the good life, consumerism encourages instant gratification, with little consideration of saving and investing for the future.

Thankfully, it's not all bad. Consumption boosts economic growth, which increases both production and employment. Living standards are generally better too. It also encourages creativity and innovation, as consumers seek improved products or services.

On the negative side, burgeoning demand for goods and services puts pressure on environmental resources, particularly water and raw materials. It also means that more energy and potentially harmful chemicals are used in mass production.

Society changes as people become more materialistic and competitive. Possessions might define people and determine their societal status. Consumerism often increases debt levels, as people resort to credit to buy what they want immediately. This can lead to mental health issues, including depression and stress. To fund their materialistic, big-spending lifestyles, people may become workaholics, sometimes at the expense of family time and relationships.

Consumerism vs Minimalism

On an individual level, the pros and cons of consumerism look a little different. Having the means to buy whatever you want is often perceived as a reward for hard work. This not only extends to material things, but may also enable a consumer to take advantage of opportunities. Consumerism fosters the misapprehension that, by purchasing more stuff, you can find satisfaction and enjoyment. Your purchasing power funds countless ways to express your uniqueness. You also have the means to spoil your loved ones, thereby expressing your affection for them.

For many individuals, however, consumerism has a dark side. It encourages people to splurge on things they can't really afford, define their self-worth in terms of their possessions, and disregard the truly valuable things in life. It is also a very wasteful lifestyle, where unwanted items are thrown away, often to make room for more. People become overwhelmed by clutter, and spend a disproportionate amount of time maintaining their possessions. They become preoccupied with things that don't really matter in the broader scheme of things—like buying a new pair of sunglasses, or the latest features of a new car model. They generally have less free time, as they need to work harder to afford their high-consumption lifestyles.

By contrast, embracing minimalism—which is often considered anti-consumption—means spending less time accumulating and maintaining material things. As you would expect, this leaves more time to spend with loved ones, enjoying meaningful experiences. People can theoretically work less, as they are not servicing huge debts and hoarding possessions. Minimalists also waste less, and their social standing is not based on what they have, but who they are. Stress is reduced, and people are happier.

However, it can be very challenging to adapt to having less possessions and fewer choices. Purging yourself of things you don't really need can be a long, labor-intensive endeavor. Very often, consumption habits are ingrained in us, and we need to consciously, significantly change the way we live to root them out.

Environmental Impacts of Consumerism

The consumer society basically takes natural resources and returns them to the environment as waste. This is a recipe for disaster. In his 1966 book *The Economics of the Coming Spaceship Earth*, economist Kenneth E Boulding famously stated: "Anyone who believes that exponential growth can go on forever in a finite world is either a madman or an economist" (AZ Quotes, n.d.).

In just thirteen years, the number of consumers will increase by two billion. Most of these will come from populous Far Eastern nations. With almost six billion consumers on the planet, demand for just about everything will spiral (The World Counts, 2020). It won't take long for us to deplete rainforests, water supplies, and even the fish in the ocean. And that's just for starters.

Our consumptive habits are already sounding alarm bells, if we would only listen. We are currently overusing the Earth's natural resources by over 70% (The World Counts, 2020). Let's take water use as an example. It takes an eye-watering 6,340 gallons of water to produce just 2.2 pounds of chocolate, 5,547 gallons to produce 2.2 pounds of coffee beans, while 4,094 produces just 2 pounds of beef. Most clothes are made in sweatshops where staff sometimes work over 100 hours a week. And the ocean will run out of seafood by 2048 if we don't call a halt to overfishing (The World Counts, 2020).

To make matters worse, most urban consumers today are completely out of touch with nature. They have little idea of the complex web of natural resources that are required to produce food; there are even people who earnestly believe that chocolate milk comes from brown cows!

Why Are So Many People Becoming Consumers?

The media tends to endorse and promote the consumer mindset. Specialists develop advertisements that convince you that your life is not as fulfilling as it should be. The solution? Purchasing a particular product, which will make you feel good.

In 1957, Vance Packard penned *The Hidden Persuaders*, a book explaining how both advertisers and politicians use psychological techniques and subliminal messaging to influence consumers. Packard says that there are eight human needs that advertisers use to sell their products. These are

- Emotional security, where consumers are promised happiness and security without any negative experiences or impacts.

- Possessing a certain product will validate your social standing, affirm your value to your community, and confirm your self-worth.

- Advertisements routinely convince buyers that they will be making good, wholesome, and wise choices, thereby pandering to the consumer's ego and need for affirmation.

- Consumers are offered products they can personalize, thereby enabling them to express their innate creativity. These include adult coloring books, or a personalized journal etched with your name.

- Everyone needs someone to love, and advertisers have the perfect love object for you—their client's products or services! Those who feel lonely or unloved in their everyday lives are more likely to fall for this type of persuasion.

- Many products are portrayed as symbols of power, which is in itself an unusually powerful motivator.

- People have different roots, or belong to a specific culture. Clever marketers who add regional twists to their campaigns encourage "locals" to feel comfortable with their offerings.

- A lot of people want to live forever, and marketers and advertisers convince us that they are our partners in staving off old age and even death.

Most people want to live lives that have meaning, and all of us want our friends and loved ones to remember us with affection when we pass away. Naturally, advertisers have homed in on this human tendency, and do their best to exploit it to their advantage.

The Power Behind the Hidden Persuaders

So how do advertisers and marketers know exactly what buttons to push to get us to do what they want? Most of the persuasive tactics that work so well were inspired by Freudian psychoanalysis. As most of us know, a Freudian slip happens when we say one thing but actually mean another. This usually happens subconsciously. It was Freud's American nephew, Edward Bernays, who turned these accidental slips into an intentional act. He called his profession "public relations counseling," but it was actually a smoke screen for propaganda.

Freud believed that humans were driven by a plethora of unconscious urges and animal instincts so powerful that they could ultimately unseat civilization as we know it. As a result, he recommended that everyone should be treated with what he termed his "talking cure." Although Freud himself was not one of the "hidden persuaders," his ideas were used—and twisted—by people who were.

At the end of World War I, Bernays and other psychoanalysts decided to focus on crowd psychology, with the aim of helping corporate America achieve its goal of maintaining the very profitable financial bases they had accumulated during the war (Massimi, 2014). Although influenced by Freud, Barnays was a force in his own right: One of his books even inspired the development of Nazi propaganda.

After the war, Bernays and his compatriots were instrumental in turning Americans into mass consumers, who purchased goods and services because they desired them, as opposed to simply needing them. This approach has underpinned most of the

Western world for almost a century (Massimi, 2014). Some analysts even believe that Roosevelt's New Deal effectively corporatized American culture, where people were considered "end users," rather than complex human beings with thoughts, feelings, and relationships with one another. At the time, the ratio between manufacturing, production, and the service industries was 9:1 in favor of manufacturing and production. The reverse is now the case (Massimi, 2014).

Corporate America was delighted with Bernays's innovations, as they were concerned that production and the wealth it had generated for them would decline once the war was over. However, Bernays was inspired and driven by far more than mere capitalist impulses. He earnestly believed that mass manipulation was the only way to control the base drives and impulses inherent in humanity and society. Not only did he justify using mass manipulation techniques to influence consumer's purchasing decisions, he also used it to sway voters toward certain political candidates.

He called this "the engineering of consent," a necessary and even desirable tool to influence people to do what his clients wanted. He believed rulers would need to quash what he called the "herd instinct," instead encouraging people to consume and behave as individuals rather than community members. After World War I, individualism came into its own, encouraged as an alternative to collaboration in order to prevent war from breaking out again (Massimi, 2014). This mass manipulation also promoted—and was fueled by—corporate greed. There was a political aspect as well. Americans were encouraged to support corporations and businesses by buying their products and services, as doing so was considered patriotic.

If you're wondering how these ideas came to be mainstream, here's a quick snapshot of the things that characterize this world view. In many ways, they epitomize our own individual experiences, so should be easy to spot.

Our overall culture today is highly focused on the self—for a very good reason. This effectively separates people from their families, friends, and communities, promoting a false "freedom," where everyone goes it alone. In a very real sense, this is divide and conquer, with the battleground being the consumer's heart, and, of course, their wallet.

Contrast this with productive communities, where many inhabitants are committed to sustainability. These communities tend to be less dependent on external goods and services than self-focused individuals. Community economies often embrace a culture of barter and gifting alongside actual monetary exchange, creating a fairer distribution of wealth. But this is anathema to the "hidden persuaders." To counter productive communities, the persuaders cultivate the myth that these rooted places are rustic, backward, and populated by conservative, uninformed people who would restrict our freedoms and smother our individuality. On the other hand, the inhabitants of these communities are encouraged to scale up and embrace the "bright lights," notwithstanding the fact that nearly all of our national policies have harmful impacts on community life and culture—but are very beneficial to corporate interests.

Cooperation of the kind often found in these sorts of communities is the antithesis of consumerism, which promotes the sort of aggressive competition where one party wins at the expense of everyone else. Hidden persuaders feed competitiveness, not only at community level, but also in our own psyches. Competitive urges make us pursue perfection, which can only be satisfied by having the latest smartphone, or a better vehicle.

The commodification of care, where institutions look after those who are ill or aged—as opposed to families looking after one another—has become big business. Many people buy into the myth that institutions who are being paid to care for people are able to do a better job than individuals would, but the truth is that we have been seduced into believing that expensive institutions are better able to care for the infirm, weaker members of society than people are. This has become a panacea for the guilt some feel at handing their loved ones over to such places.

Both individuals and communities have given outsiders and complete strangers the power to decide where and how they will spend their income. This runs counter to people taking stock of their needs and making purchasing decisions accordingly. The persuaders of course strongly assert that only buying their products or services will enable the purchasers to have better lives. Community, neighborliness, friendship, and family are all brushed aside as though they were of no account.

Associations generally enable people and communities to pool their time, talents, and resources, which enables skills and time to be bartered among members. However, associations only function properly in a non-hierarchical gift economy, which is difficult to achieve in today's world. These associations therefore tend to be very susceptible to outside forces. Propagandists will very often find a niche they can exploit, providing what appears to be a necessary service, which in reality, actually helps to further their ultimate goals.

Don't be surprised if you have been living in blissful ignorance for years. The hidden persuaders are often masked, hiding their true agendas from one another, and even from themselves. Some of them are genuinely convinced that they are acting in society's best interests by removing individuals from "the herd," and encouraging them to become their best selves.

Escaping the Consumption Trap

Many people caught on the treadmill of consumerism and consumption are unhappy. This is because they're investing in a lifestyle that doesn't allow them any time to think beyond their possessions. They are unable to spend time with people who matter to them because they're always chasing some elusive consumerist Holy Grail, and they're prevented from focusing on aspects of life that might be more fulfilling, such as pursuing a hobby or interest, making things, spending time with friends, or tending a garden.

Consumerism is all about fulfilling your desires, whereas minimalism focuses on what you need. Through advertising, consumers are convinced that a certain product will offer a panacea for a particular need or desire, whereas in reality, it will do nothing of the sort. After a brief "feel good" moment, the thing you've purchased will become another item of clutter in your home, confined to a basement storeroom.

The minimalist approach to the lure of advertising and the urge to consume is simple. First, stop and ask the question, "Do I really need this?" This approach can help minimalists—and those who simply wish to reduce their consumption—dodge the fake promises implicit in most advertisements and promotions today. If you do this often enough, it will become a habit, and your life will be richer and more satisfying for it.

In case you're wondering, being a minimalist doesn't mean that you need to become poverty-stricken. What it *does* mean is that you are able to control those impulses—carefully honed by the media and advertising gurus—to spend lavishly. You don't need to sell everything and live like a hermit in a jungle—unless you're a missionary and have been specifically called to that kind of life. What it means is not spending money on things you don't really need, and only spending where necessary. By acquiring only the things that you need, you won't need to accumulate expensive things to cultivate a sense of self-worth.

Transitioning from Consumerism to Minimalism: First Steps

It isn't easy to resist the messages our consumer culture continually throws at us: "Get this, buy that, act now, you need this, keep up with the Joneses..." But you must resist them if you are to experience improved quality of life as an anti-consumer. It takes time to develop a minimalist mindset but, like most things in life, you can succeed if you really want to.

Here is a quick "how-to" guide to help you achieve minimalism:

- First, think hard about your possessions: What do you really need and what is just clutter? List the things you actually need and those you simply would like to have. This will help you differentiate between luxuries and necessities.

- Selling or passing on items you don't need is a good starting point. Giving to charity will make you feel good. If you sell things, that extra cash can be kept for a rainy day. You might even open a savings account with it.

- Be conscious of your impulses. What things do you desire the most? Do you shop more when you are unhappy or depressed? Do you buy lots of things you don't need and regret it afterward?

- Before you buy things, carefully consider whether you really need them. If you do this regularly, you'll find that you'll eventually do it automatically. Pressing your personal pause button will prevent you from mindlessly spending lots of money on trivial things. The desire for that item you thought you couldn't live without may very well fade away when you do this. If it doesn't, and you still think you should purchase the item, then do so.

- Ignore advertisements. Considering the degree to which we're bombarded with everything from highway billboards to television and media advertising; this is easier said than done. To avoid seeing too many cleverly crafted appeals to spend, limit the time you spend on social media and watching television. This will also afford you more peace and tranquility.

- Practice delayed gratification, and make yourself wait. Give yourself plenty of time to think before making purchasing decisions. Consider the essence, benefits, and necessity of the purchase you are about to make, as well as any downsides, such as maintenance requirements, durability, and recyclability.

While transitioning to minimalism may be somewhat challenging, depending on how acquisitive you are, it can be done. The practice will enable you to distinguish actual needs from wants and desires, enabling you to let go of the things you don't actually need. The above practices will help you do that.

Chapter 6:
How to Be a Minimalist

The minimalist lifestyle can be encapsulated by the phrase "less is more." Much like sustainable living, it asks us to reduce how much we buy. While sustainable living encourages us to consume less, minimalism offers another solution for a sustainable future, as long as those who embrace this lifestyle take it far enough to actually reduce their environmental footprints.

The central theme of minimalism is to accumulate less stuff, reducing clutter and avoiding mindless consumption. This results in happier people who have more time, are more focused, and productive. This in itself may be a motivating factor for people exploring minimalist lifestyles. When combined with an ecological consciousness, it multiplies the positive impact on the planet.

Minimalism Explained

Recently, I was listening to a morning radio show while driving. It was the end of the month, and the DJ said to his co-host—and us, the listeners—"Well, today, I'm feeling good. I've got money in the bank. Maybe I'll have myself a nice dinner tonight.

But tomorrow, when those debit orders come off, I'm not going to be so well off. I'll be lucky to make it to the end of the month."

Most people live from paycheck to paycheck, very often with no extra money for doing things they enjoy, or spending time with special people they love. Their lives are defined by the morning and evening commutes, the nine-to-five grind, and rush hour traffic. Come the weekend, it's Friday evening or Saturday morning shopping, and weekend chores, with some online movies thrown in. No wonder we have blue Mondays. For many, it's enough to simply exist. Most people drift through life in this haphazard fashion, vaguely hoping that things will get better, without really doing anything to change their situations. As a society, drowning in debt and burdened with unnecessary possessions, we have lost the art of living intentionally.

And that's the very essence of minimalism. It's all the rage now, but actively choosing to become minimalist, and maintaining that lifestyle, isn't a random decision, or a passing phase. It's deliberately focusing on what we value the most, and removing everything that distances us from it. Besides the obvious, minimalism will teach you habits that you will find beneficial in other areas of your life, resulting in overall improvements.

As discussed in the previous chapter, minimalism liberates its practitioners from consumption—and from the quest to possess every desirable thing they see. Material goods can't grant us our deepest, most heartfelt human needs: real relationships, genuine experiences, and opportunities to nourish our souls. Minimalists appreciate all they have, which spawns gratitude, thus enabling them to have a more abundant life without the encumbrances of possessions.

Many years ago, a friend told me about a humorous bumper sticker she saw: "The rat race is over. The rats won." Many of us live as though the rats are after us. The modern world is a paradoxical contradiction in terms, rushing by like a bullet train we can't seem to disembark. We're constantly hurried and stressed. We may work long hours—and our debt burden mounts. We are in constant motion, yet seem to get nothing done. We are always in touch with others through our smartphones, yet real connections remain elusive.

Minimalism forces people to take their time with things, enabling them to delink from the rapid and accelerating pace of modern life. There is time to opt out and disengage for as long as you wish. By possessing only the essentials, minimalists focus on what is significant, intentionally adding value to their lives.

Today's society has forgotten how to be genuine. There is no loyalty: People switch allegiances with startling alacrity. Others hide their real selves behind fake smiles, displaying different characteristics—depending on the occasion—or the person they are dealing with at a particular time. This all changes when you adopt a simpler life, which yields consistency and unity. No matter what the circumstances, the person and their values remain the same. There is honesty, transparency, and dependability.

Unlike many people who idolize celebrities, chasing after success, recognition, and excitement, minimalism invites us to not only decelerate and reduce our consumption, but to enjoy the tranquility of a quieter, less complicated life. Minimalism, at its core, is about finding the things the human heart truly seeks, and embracing them to live life to the fullest.

Striking A Balance

Taken to extremes, consumerism can leave people penniless and empty, always chasing after something they can't quite seem to find, and trapping them in a never-ending cycle of pointlessness and frustration. Extreme minimalism is also not for the faint-hearted. While paring down your possessions to the bare minimum is a basic tenet of minimalism, there are no rules, and it's up to you how far you want to extend yourself.

Perhaps the best way of establishing what your minimalist threshold is, is to review all the areas of your life you consider important, and decide whether these would benefit from minimizing. Alternatively, you might already be prepared to embark on this life-changing journey.

Decluttering Made Easy

To begin your foray into minimalism, you will most likely need to start by decluttering your home. Depending on the amount of stuff you have accumulated, this might seem to be a daunting task. To make things easier, I have compiled a list of decluttering suggestions to get you started.

Linen Closet

- Torn sheets and worn-out bed pillows
- Rags (reduce your collection)
- Excess small appliances, e.g. irons, steamers, etc)
- Dead batteries (Contact Call2Recycle: www.call2recycle.org)
- Household cleaning supplies
- Comforters
- Linen sets

- Duvets

- Blankets

- Towels

- Items from another life phase, e.g. college

Office

- Shred all old or unneeded documents

- Old, torn, or tattered manilla file folders

- Pens and pencils (decide on a number)

- Items on your bulletin board

- Magnets

- Home office supplies

- Coins

- Rubber bands

- Excess pads of paper or envelopes

- Reduce your scrap paper to what you'll actually use

- Old stationery you no longer like

- Check the balances and validity of old gift cards and coupons

- Outdated digital cameras

- Old business cards—yours or other people's

- Books you won't read again

- Excess USB drives—remember to check and delete the contents first

- Trade show freebies you don't want or use

- Computer equipment

- Computer peripherals

- Charging, computer, and phone cords

Kitchen

- Expired or stale food

- Food that is still edible that you can donate

- Single-use utensils and plates that you don't need

- Expired spices or spices you never use

- Panty organizers you never use

- Excess plastic or reusable bags

- Clean out the fridge—toss all expired food and wipe down the shelves

- Excess cooking utensils

- Excess sauce packets and takeout items

- Extra bread ties and twist ties

- Appliances you never use

- Kitchen glassware

- Cookbooks

- Kitchen gadgets

- Mixing bowls

- Tupperware and plastic containers

- Water pitchers

- Coffee mugs

- Glass jars

- Excess serving platters and hosting items

- Excess barware

- Dishware you inherited but don't use

- Old, dirty dish towels

- Cleaning supplies you don't use

- Fridge magnets you don't like

- Cleaning sponges—you only need a few in use

- Extra or unmatched food containers

Bedroom

- Paper clutter on surfaces

- Create a place for loose change

- Random items under the bed

- Too many books next to the bed

- Go through all clothing in dressers

- Declutter your bedside table

- Excess hats

- Handbags you don't use

- Thin out your T-shirt collection

- Pants and shorts

- Dresses and skirts

- Ties, belts, and accessories

- Winter clothing and accessories

- Excess socks and underwear

- Sleepwear

- Jewelry

- Shoes you never wear

- Excess hangers, including wire hangers

- Coats and jackets

- Excess scarves

- Swimsuits that are worn out or dated

- Broken or old sunglasses

- Sentimental items

- Decor that is no longer to your taste or is outdated

- Formal items you won't wear again

Bathroom

- Old or expired makeup and brushes

- Old or expired sunscreen

- Excess hair brushes and tools

- Worn out hair ties or bobby pins

- Beauty products you don't use or like

- Dried out or separated nail polish

- Unused beauty or travel samples

- Cleaning products you tried but don't like

- Expired over-the-counter medicine

- Personal beauty appliances

- Toiletries

Children

- Broken toys

- Toys your children don't like or have outgrown

- Dried up markers

- Games and puzzles with missing pieces

- Declutter collections, such as Barbies and Legos

- Used-up coloring or activity books

- Dried out Play Doh

- Dress-up costumes that no longer fit

- Baby clothes and supplies

- Old school books and papers

- Stuffed animals

- Children's artwork

Pets

- Old or broken pet's toys, or toys they aren't interested in anymore

- Pet clothes that no longer fit

- Pet treats they don't eat anymore or which have expired

- Pet grooming items you no longer use

- Expired pet medications

- Old food and water bowls

Entertainment and Miscellaneous

- Magazines and newspapers

- Photographs

- Photography equipment and supplies

- Sewing supplies

- Scrapbooking supplies

- Other craft supplies

- CDs

- DVDs and VHS tapes

- Wall decorations

- Used candles and old candle holders

- Figurines

- Crystal and china

- Vases

- Audiovisual components and cables

- Old cell phones

- Furniture

- Video game systems, games, and accessories

- Televisions

- Coolers

- Manuals

- Phone books

- Coupons

- Board games and puzzles

- Decks of cards

- Unused gifts

- Suitcases

- Paper goods

- Wrapping supplies

- Plastic bags

- Party supplies

Garage

- Tools

- Hardware

- Seasonal decorations

- Sporting goods

- Sports memorabilia

- Automotive supplies

- Scrap pieces of lumber

- Brooms

- Rakes

- Shovels

- Garden tools

- Plant containers and pots

- Empty cardboard boxes

- Old car parts (or project cars you won't finish)

Thrift Shops

Once you have done some decluttering, you'll very likely end up with a pile of things you no longer need or want. Getting rid of it all can be a problem—but you can always donate it to a thrift shop. There is more to this than simply loading up the trunk of your car and arriving at their doors, though. Here's a quick guide on donating to thrift shops:

- Before giving to a thrift shop, consider people you know who might like to have the items you no longer want, and ask them first (or join a Buy Nothing group, discussed in the next section.)

- If you have any broken items, or things that no longer work, chances are that a thrift shop wouldn't want them either. Consider repairing or recycling these items.

- Thrift shops won't be happy with broken or chipped glassware, and broken or stained furniture, either.

- Visit the thrift shops and charities in your area, and find out what items they are looking for. It may be more work, but your clutter has less chance of ending up in a landfill that way, as some thrift shops still throw out unwanted or unsuitable items.

- While thrift shops have different niches and needs, clothing is often in high demand.
- In some areas, thrift shop customers may prefer quality housewares.

- Do not donate weapons, including hunting knives and ammunition. If you have hazardous chemicals, paint, electronics, and scrap metal, dispose of them properly. Some landfills have special sections that accept these materials.

Items that you can donate to most thrift shops include the following:

- Clothing, including shoes, gloves, hats, and scarves
- Jewelry
- Bags
- Pre-loved books
- Housewares, together with pots and pans, dishes, china, and flatware
- Board games and toys
- DVDs and CDs
- Computers and electronic goods
- Furniture and antiques

The "Buy Nothing" Philosophy

The Black Friday sale epitomizes how obsessed our societies have become with the accumulation of material possessions. It's ironic to think that the marketing gurus have timed it to fall immediately after Thanksgiving, a celebration of gratitude—and we are encouraged to rush out and buy more things the very next day. This mega sale, which has now been taken up by many countries and retailers across the world, has become another reason to spend, spend, and spend. Shoppers line up well before dawn on Black Friday, charging into stores the minute the doors open, and grabbing a wide variety of goods, as though they have never seen television sets, appliances, liquor, clothing, or groceries before.

The first time I heard about the Buy Nothing movement was when memes popped up on my social media feeds, encouraging readers to go on nature walks, spend time with friends, or read a good book instead of racing to the nearest shopping mall on Black Friday. I thought this was a wonderful idea—and I still do. Living in a rural area and not being much of a shopper by inclination probably has something to do with it, though.

The Buy Nothing project was started by Liesl Clark and Rebecca Rockefeller in Washington (Fenton, 2022). The pair wanted to develop a hyper-local gift economy in their community, creating a platform where neighbors could give things away, share, or lend to one another. It became so successful that it's practically a global movement these days.

While each community has its own rules, the one that is non-negotiable is that nothing should be bought, sold, or bartered. Everything must be given freely, and some groups even prohibit mentioning the monetary value of the items listed. People are encouraged to join local groups, so that they can give to their local communities.

Buy Nothing groups are wonderful places to find free stuff—and offload your clutter if you haven't been able to sell items secondhand. In fact, some members would rather post items they no longer want or need to their local Buy Nothing group than send them to thrift stores or charity shops. Quality items in need of repair might also find a home in Buy Nothing groups. Many Buy Nothing members find giving much more rewarding—and a lot easier—than trying to sell unwanted items secondhand. And those who give receive too, so it's a win-win.

The Buy Nothing movement is also about giving one's talents, abilities, and time. This can include things like free ride shares, tutoring, or being a workout buddy. After a heavy New York snowstorm, Buy Nothing members got out their shovels and cleared neighborhood streets for free.

While the Buy Nothing project is a great community group to get involved in, there are a couple of do's and don'ts. Members need to be honest about the condition of the goods they are offering. Be prepared for some surprises: A tinkerer might be able to fix your broken kettle, and someone might even want that half-used box of laundry detergent you no longer need. Members are advised to give everyone in the group a chance to request popular items instead of giving them to the first person who inquires. If you want something but then change your mind, be sure to tell the gifter. Members are encouraged to communicate quickly and effectively, so that the gift can be given without delay.

If you're interested in finding out more about Buy Nothing or the gift economy, you can take a class with the Buy Nothing Academy. This can equip you to start your own Buy Nothing group, or even begin a similar initiative. There is also an app to help you get started. Another option is to either start or join a local Facebook group. This might split into smaller groups over time, but that's okay. It means more people are getting involved in the gift economy.

There's another type of waste that's not necessarily resolved by going minimalist, although it forms one of the largest components of the U.S. waste stream, and is a problem in many other parts of the world too. That's food. In the next chapter, you'll discover how serious the issue is and how to deal with your food waste.

Chapter 7:
Food Waste and Contamination

If you were a picky eater as a child, you'll probably remember your mother insisting that you eat all your greens, because there was a family in Africa going hungry, and they'd be glad to have them. I was a picky eater when I was a child, and this was a constant refrain in our family. Food waste is a growing problem in all countries, and at all levels of society.

According to the World Food Program, around 1.4 billion tons of food is wasted every year, valued at around one trillion U.S. dollars. Nearly a third of all the food produced globally is lost before it is even consumed. The demographics of food waste are also different depending on where in the world people live: People in rich nations waste the most—equivalent to the entire net food production of sub-Saharan Africa annually, while in developing countries, forty percent of losses occur after harvest and during processing (World Food Programme, 2020).

But the issue of food waste is about much more than people going hungry. In the U.S., food waste makes up the largest proportion of waste in landfills at around 22%, and the average American wastes 50% more food than they did in 1970 (Center for Sustainable Systems, 2021). Americans generate around 80 billion pounds of food waste a year, representing around 30–40% of the nation's entire food supply. About 80% of people in the U.S. throw away edible food, largely because of confusion around expiration dates (Eco.Logic, n.d.).

The problem is, that when this food ends up in landfills rather than being composted, it contributes to the methane generated when the waste in the landfill decomposes. Methane is a particularly potent greenhouse gas. Wasting food contributes to 11% of global greenhouse gas emissions (Eco.Logic, n.d.).

Food waste is generated by food manufacturers, farms, restaurants, grocery stores, and within people's homes. The latter two sources are as high as 40% (Eco.Logic, n.d.).

Earlier in this book, we looked at a number of things individuals can do to reduce the amount of plastic they use. In the same way, there is a solution to the food waste issue. Best of all, it mimics the way nature recycles materials, a system known as biomimicry. This is composting, and it's the process of turning food—and garden waste—into a nutritious additive your garden plants and vegetables will love.

Why Compost?

While both landfills and composting will break down food waste, the process is rather different. Organic matter in a landfill decomposes anaerobically, in other words, without using oxygen. However, in nature (and a compost heap), organic waste decomposes aerobically, in other words, with oxygen. When food breaks down anaerobically, it produces greenhouse gasses such as methane, thereby contributing to carbon emissions and climate change. Municipal solid waste landfills in the U.S. are the third-largest emitter of human-related methane gas in the nation (Addison County, 2019).

Adding organic matter like compost to soil improves its structure and texture, ensuring the healthy growth of plants. When more organic matter is present in the soil, the soil is better able to retain water, nutrients, and air. This creates better growing conditions, which benefits the entire system. For instance, increasing the soil's organic matter by just 1% improves the soil's water holding capacity three-fold (Addison County, 2019).

Plants receiving regular compost applications are stronger, healthier, and better able to resist pests and diseases. This reduces the need for toxic pesticides. In addition, compost releases nutrients slowly, as the different materials in compost break down at different rates. Compost contains more nutrients than fertilizers, as it is sourced from a wide diversity of materials. This means that the need for fertilizer is also reduced.

Food that is thrown away contains many essential vitamins and nutrients, which were taken up by the plant while it was growing. When these nutrients are composted, they are returned to the soil, recycled back into the ecosystem, and taken up again when the next crop is grown on the land. Composting is a great way to recycle nutrients naturally.

Compost also attracts beneficial creatures and microorganisms, which are good for both the soil and the plants that grow in it. It's a bit like a probiotic for your garden, as it contains lots of beneficial bacteria that not only make plants grow, but improve the health of your garden ecosystem too. Healthy soil contains a community of beneficial organisms that break down organic matter, improve soil structure, and create a fertile environment for plants.

How to Compost

Making your own compost isn't difficult—after all, nature does all the hard work for you! How you make compost is up to you. You can have a simple rot pile, where you toss vegetable peelings and other kitchen waste, leaves, garden prunings, old newspapers, and other compostable materials. A rot pile shouldn't be higher than about three feet, so you can easily mix it. It should also be compact enough to retain heat (SOS Future, 2020).

Or you could invest in a compost bin. Compost bins are made of a variety of materials. If you are going zero waste, you can opt for a wooden one, which will eventually break down as well. Make sure it's easy to rotate, so you can turn it and mix your compost up (this helps to speed up the breakdown process as well).

A container can sit on top of the soil or be buried part-way. Ensure that it has small drainage holes in the bottom and sides to let air in and water out. It might also need a cover to keep out flies, rats, and other pests, and to ensure that the compost does not become saturated during heavy rains.

You can make your own compost bin from repurposed materials rather than buying one. Use wooden pallets (make sure the wood has not been treated with pesticides or painted), an old storage container or utility box, a garbage can, a stack of milk crates (three is a good number), or an old wine barrel. If you want to have a countertop bin to keep your kitchen waste before throwing it onto the heap, you can use an empty glass jar, or a coffee container (The Daily Gardener, 2020).

Location

Compost is actually waste and might give off unpleasant smells at times as the waste breaks down to become this amazing garden amendment. So you don't want any odors to assail your nose— or your visitors' noses—every time you walk out the door. Choose a place out of reach of foraging animals, including feral cats, and with enough exposure to the air to ensure that your heap is aerated sufficiently. The heap should be close to shade (but should not be shaded all day), and near a water point, as it needs to be watered regularly if there is no rainfall to ensure that the waste breaks down properly. Don't let your heap encroach on the trunks of trees either, as it will rot the trees.

Choose a well-drained spot. If you wish, you can dig a hole in the ground, about one and a half feet deep, and any width you like (Seema, 2019).

Separation and Composting Methods

If you are eager to start composting, it will be essential for you to separate your organic waste from your inorganic waste.

Organic waste refers to anything that was once alive, or is derived from a living organism, such as your vegetable peelings or garden clippings. Inorganic waste refers to things like plastic, metal, or glass items.

There are basically two ways of creating a compost heap. Which one you choose essentially depends on how patient you are:

- The first is what's known as the "hot" compost method—and this one is recommended for impatient gardeners. Here you need the right balance of organic matter that is both carbon-and-nitrogen-rich. Turn it once a week, as this helps to aerate the heap, introducing oxygen regularly to keep the decomposition rate high. This method is very labor-intensive, but produces very quick results.

- The second method is known as the "cold" method, and is ideal for those who don't want to turn their heap continuously (or if you have a very large heap, which is impractical to keep turning all the time.) The compost takes longer to mature, but is very rich in microorganisms compared to the "hot" method, which is driven by bacteria.

What to Compost

Compost should ideally contain both carbon-rich materials ("browns"), as well as nitrogen-rich materials (or "greens").

Examples of "browns" include dried plant material, dried leaves, dried grass clippings, dried garden trimmings, hay, straw, wood shavings, sawdust, coconut hulls, and twigs. Kitchen waste that can be categorized as "browns" includes all dried organic material, such as wood ash, cardboard, egg cartons, paper towels, newspaper, and even vacuum cleaner dust.

"Greens" consist of any fresh organic material derived from both the garden and kitchen. Examples include spent vegetables and flowers, old fruit, hedge trimmings, fresh grass clippings, seaweed, and manures, as well as fruit and vegetable peels, egg shells, coffee grounds, used tea bags and tea leaves, sour milk, pet hair, and moderate amounts of citrus peel.

What Not To Compost

There are some materials that should never be added to the compost heap—and can in fact be very detrimental. These include deep fried food, tin cans, cloths, clothes, paint and used paint brushes, glass, glossy magazines, coal ash, disposable diapers, containers that might have held poisonous dust, diseased plants, timber or sawdust from chemically treated wood, or painted wood, pesticide-or herbicide-sprayed plant material, glue, plastic containers, old oil, and detergents.

Don't add any cooked food or bones from fish or livestock to your compost bin or heap. There is a caveat, however. If you use bokashi to break them down first, then the resultant brew can be added to the heap.

Bokashi is Japanese for "fermented organic matter." The process involves layering kitchen waste like vegetable, fruit, meat, and dairy scraps in a special bucket and adding a bokashi inoculant. The latter has a wheat germ, wheat bran, or sawdust base combined with molasses and effective microorganisms (EM). The bran and molasses feed the microorganisms, which are the same as the ones found in nature. Initially, a liquid is produced, which can be fed to plants as bokashi tea. When layered and left in a shady place, the mixture ferments rapidly. Within as little as 10 days, it can be dug into the garden or added to a traditional compost pile to finish breaking down (Vanderlinden, 2022).

In regards to manure, it is best not to add pig manure, dog droppings, cat litter, human excrement, or sewage farm slurry. These contain pathogens that could cause disease. In addition, cattle manure is best avoided, as it may be tainted with growth hormones and antibiotics. Always establish the source of the manure before you buy it.

Monitor Your Compost

Check your compost often to ensure that it stays warm, as this will continue the composting process. This will also enable you to determine when the compost should be mixed or turned. Use your hands or a thermometer to check the temperature. If the compost heap or bin was warm and then turned cold, give it a good turning to restart the process. The compost also needs to stay moist, and get enough oxygen so the bacteria continue their important decomposition work. Use a pitchfork to turn your heap. Moisten dry materials like sawdust or dead leaves when adding them to the heap.

When Will the Compost Be Ready?

Cover your rot pile or bin with a tarp to keep it moist. Look at the bottom of the heap to see if your compost is ready. It should be a dark, rich color. This may take anything from a few weeks to months.

If you have a large rot pile and are using the "cold" composting method, the compost will take about a year to mature. Turn the heap in the fall to liberate the compost underneath. Use the remaining materials to begin the next year's heap.

How to Prevent Food Waste at Home

As mentioned previously, our homes generate a startling amount of food waste. It's essential to avoid wasting food in the first place, even if you can recover some of this waste through composting. There are other benefits to reducing food waste too:

- Did you know that the average family of four spends around $1,500 every year on food they never eat (U.S. EPA, 2013)? Buying only what you need, and eating everything you buy will save you money straight away. You also won't throw food away—and the monetary savings can be used for something else that you need.

- Food waste is about more than food. What's also wasted are all the inputs that went into producing it: the land, water, energy, production, food processing, transport, preparing, storing, and disposal. Reducing or eliminating food waste in your household will help to conserve all these resources and energy.

- More than 85% of greenhouse gas emissions from food waste that ends up in landfills results from what happened to the food before it got there, including production, transport, processing, and distribution (U.S. EPA, 2013).

Ways to Prevent Food Waste at Home

A Note About "Best By," "Sell By," and "Use By" Dates

- The "best by" date indicates when a food product will have the best flavor or quality, so the flavor and texture will be optimal when consumed within and by these dates.

- "Sell by" dates are specific to the particular grocery store, and are determined by how long they can have items on the shelves and for sale. These foods should be refrigerated or frozen once you get them home, but they are still safe to consume and should be of good quality beyond the "sell by" date.

- The "use by" date is the last day that the manufacturer recommends consuming the product. This is mainly for quality reasons as opposed to food safety. However, as it's the last day of a product's peak quality, you might not want to extend it too far.

Buying Food

- If you're the cook in your home, list the meals and their ingredients that your family really enjoys, to ensure that you're preparing meals that everyone will eat.

- Always check your refrigerator and pantry or cupboards before going food shopping to avoid buying food you already have at home. Each week, make a list of things that need to be used up, and plan your meals around them.

- Plan your weekly meals beforehand, and only shop for ingredients for those meals. When you make your list, consider things like how often you will be eating at home that week. Visiting friends, eating takeout or pre-made meals, or going out to eat will all reduce how much food you'll use in a particular week.

- Consider whether you'll have enough leftovers from a meal to use for a second meal on another evening, or freeze for a time when you will get home too late to cook.

- Avoid overbuying by deciding beforehand how much you need to buy for a particular meal.

- Only buy in large quantities if you will eat all the food. Two-for-one and bulk buy specials are only cost-effective if you don't waste any of the food. Having said that, buying in bulk can both save you money and reduce the amount of packaging you consume.

- Store food correctly to prevent it from spoiling, e.g. pack it in airtight containers, re-pack it into meal-size portions and freeze it, or dry it if you have a dehydrator.

- Purchase imperfect fresh produce or upcycled products. Imperfect produce is just as nutritious, while upcycled products are made from ingredients that could have gone to waste.

Storing Food

- Most vegetables, especially those that wilt, such as lettuce, celery, and cucumber, should go into the high humidity drawer of your refrigerator.

- Fruits and vegetables that age quickly, such as mushrooms and peppers, should go into the low humidity drawer.

- Store fruits that ripen quickly, such as bananas, apples, pears, stone fruits, and avocados away from other fruits. Ripe fruit releases ethylene gas, which makes other fruit and vegetables ripen faster.

- Only wash cherries, berries, and grapes when you are ready to eat them so that they don't go moldy.

- Potatoes, eggplants, winter squash, onions, and garlic should be stored in a cool, dry, dark and well-ventilated place to keep for as long as possible.

- The refrigerator door is the warmest part of the fridge, ideal for storing condiments. Don't store eggs or milk there, as they will deteriorate quicker.

- The lower shelves are the coldest and should be used for meat, poultry, and fish.

- Set your refrigerator to maintain a temperature of 40°F or less.

- Store grains in airtight containers and remember to label them with the date.

- Freezing is still a great way to store food. Freeze bread, sliced fruit, meat, or leftover food. Label containers with the contents and the date (you can reuse old margarine tubs for this purpose).

Cooking and Preparing Food

- Fresh produce that is past its prime, as well as the last remnants of ingredients or even leftovers may still be fine for cooking. Use them in soups, stews, casseroles, stir fries, and more.

- Use foods that you wouldn't normally eat, as long as this will be safe and healthy. For example, make croutons with stale bread, and use vegetable scraps such as sauteed beet greens to make soup stocks.

- Understand the difference between "sell by," "use by," and the expiration dates on food labels.

- Cook and serve the right portions for the number of people who will be eating.

- Preserve fruits and vegetables by freezing, pickling, dehydrating, canning, or making jams and jellies.

- Don't leave perishable food at room temperature for longer than two hours (U.S. EPA, 2013).

Other Ways to Avoid Food Waste

Besides composting, extra food can be donated to food banks to help those in need.

A Double Bonus: Reducing Food Waste *and* Packaging Waste

In the European Union, some 100 million tons of food (about 30% of agricultural production) is wasted annually. It is anticipated that this could double by 2050, while global food supplies would need to increase by 50% (Guillard et al., 2018). One of the reasons why so much food is wasted is because fresh produce in particular has a very short shelf life. About 20% of edible food is thrown out due to misunderstanding food labels (Guillard et al., 2018).

Considering the way food is packaged should be part of sustainable food consumption. Correctly packaged food has a longer shelf life, which means that it won't spoil as quickly and be wasted. Packaging should ideally be regarded as an aid to reducing waste rather than an economic and environmental cost.

When food is thrown away, so is its packaging. This leads to a double burden, as much packaging is made from plastic, produced in turn from oil. Around 23 million metric tons of plastic are produced annually in Europe, which is expected to increase to 92 million tons by 2050. Food packaging is used for a very short time, and as much as 40% may end up in landfills (Guillard et al., 2018).

The Bioplastic Alternative

Researchers and manufacturers have been considering alternative raw materials other than plastic for packaging for some time. The word "bioplastic" is actually used interchangeably to refer to two different things: bio-based plastics (plastic made at least partly from natural substances), and biodegradable plastics (plastic that microbes break down within a reasonably short space of time). The reality is that not all bio-based plastics are biodegradable, and not all biodegradable plastics are made with natural raw materials.

Most of the former bioplastic options have been based on cornstarch and cane sugar. This has consequences for human food requirements, as corn is a staple in many parts of the world. Deriving bioplastics from such resources also increases the need for agricultural land.

You'll be surprised to learn that, despite the hype, most of these bioplastics are not compostable, or can only be composted in industrial systems. This means that bioplastic items need to be specially collected and sorted, creating a waste management headache. Getting consumers to accept more sustainable packaging options is also difficult because the links between alternative packaging and the environmental improvements they create are often not very obvious, and producers may be accused of greenwashing.

Sustainable food packaging reduces the likelihood of food loss and waste because this ensures food quality and safety, especially when food is distributed and consumed. The packaging is actually just as important as the food it contains. The two are interlinked, and should be considered together when food waste and packaging solutions are being considered.

Quality food packaging preserves food integrity and safety, and reduces food waste and food-borne diseases. Researchers have been focusing on developing bioplastics from organic waste, such as crop residues, agro-food by-products, and similar feedstocks. The idea is to promote a circular economy concept that allows for proper food consumption, while avoiding the plastic packaging minefield. Unsurprisingly, considering the concern over our ever-increasing accumulation of plastic waste, interest in bio-packaging is growing throughout the world. Despite this, the market is still very small due to there being technical difficulties associated with the production and quality of plastic alternatives made with natural raw materials.

It goes without saying that converting agricultural residues into "naturally biodegradable" packaging would provide tangible environmental, economic, and industrial benefits. There are already natural polymers available that could substitute those traditionally used for plastic production—but they are still prohibitively expensive, and manufacturers are reluctant to use them.

If bioplastics were to become commercially and economically viable, 50% of European food packaging materials could be produced from renewable feedstocks (Guillard et al., 2018).

But Are Bioplastics the Answer?

For some plastics, the same polymer chains can be used from renewable resources. Polyethylene Terephthalate (PET) plastic, which you will remember has a recycle number of one, is particularly suitable for bioplastics. However, even if PET items are made from sugarcane waste, for example, they would still persist in the environment for years. In addition, none of the standards for bioplastics allow them to be disposed of in the natural environment. So, are bioplastics a real solution to humanity's plastic waste problem, or do they just make us feel better about it?

Produced from cane sugar or potato starch, polylactic acid (PLA) is used in shopping bags, transparent cups, 3-D printing materials, and several other items. The good news is that it is recyclable, biodegradable, and compostable. But that doesn't mean it can be discarded just anywhere. For example, drinking straws made with PLA won't biodegrade on beaches, or even in the sea. PLA is one of the plastics that can only be industrially composted at temperatures of over 136 °F (Krieger, 2019).

Other bioplastics may, however, degrade in marine environments. Derived from microbes, polyhydroxyalkanoates (PHA) will break down on a tropical seafloor in just two or three months, but, in the Mediterranean, this might take ten times longer (Krieger, 2019). And, in very cold regions, they might take an extremely long time to biodegrade. At the moment, PHA has a tiny market share, but this is likely to increase.

Even with the best waste management systems, some plastic might still escape. So, can completely biodegradable plastic be created? Some researchers say that it is possible to build molecular triggers into objects so that they "know" when to start breaking down. This idea is expensive and unwieldy, as scientists would need to build triggers for a massive array of items, which would be impractical and impossible.

Not only that, biodegradable plastics can also have negative impacts on the natural world. Just like regular plastic, bioplastics can cause oxidative stress or disturb hormone production in natural organisms. The chemicals used to make bioplastics may turn out to be just as harmful as those used in conventional plastic.

Another problem with biobased plastics is the issue of finding enough land to grow the crops required. While some researchers believe that bioplastics won't interfere with food production and security, not everyone agrees. Besides the challenge of needing to find more arable land to use for bioplastic production, these crops will likely be grown as monocultures, using large quantities of pesticides. There may also be issues around biodiversity, water availability and contamination, and desertification. These impacts could be mitigated if manufacturers reused waste bioplastics or used non-agricultural feedstocks.

Plastics marketed today as biodegradable will still end up littering the countryside or taking up space in landfills, because they take a long time to disappear completely. Accordingly, they could impact wildlife and ecosystems in much the same way as regular plastic does. Having said that, there are some uses for them, such as bags that are used to collect organic waste in some countries. These bags can also be used to collect food scraps for composting. This prevents organics from ending up in the trash, which means less fermentation, and trash could be collected less often. This could not only save money, but make it easier to sift out recyclable materials, such as paper, glass, aluminum, and similar items, as recyclables would be less likely to be contaminated. On the down side, many countries don't yet have the infrastructure to screen for biodegradable plastics.

Having said that, biodegradable plastic bags can be used as mulch in agricultural settings. This could replace mulch films currently being used, which are made of conventional plastic, and need to be removed and discarded to prevent soils from becoming contaminated with chemicals.

If you want to purchase biodegradable plastic, check the label carefully to establish how easily it degrades, and how you should dispose of it. You also need to be aware that there are fake labels out there too. Then there are oxo-biodegradable materials, which are conventional plastics mixed with minerals to make them break down quicker. There are two problems with this: There is no proof that these types of plastics degrade faster, and they might simply turn into microplastics.

This means that the best option for tackling our plastic waste problem is still to reduce or eliminate the amount of plastic we use.

In the next chapter, you'll find out about yet another way to embrace minimalism and use less planetary resources, besides saving money and enabling more personal freedom to spend time doing the things that are important to you, as well as building good relationships with other people. We're going to take a look at a trend that is slowly but surely gaining traction across the globe—tiny houses.

Chapter 8:
Living in a Tiny House

A friend of mine knows a couple who decided to settle down after many years of being nomadic, traveling around the country in a campervan. Now they have a young child, and decided that they wanted to stay in one place. But they didn't want to have a life encumbered by stuff. They chose to sink some funds into a plot of land on the coast, in an unspoiled area that appealed to them. Then they got down to business. Using waste lumber and various other items that are normally scrapped—old doors, bits of window glass, old light fittings, and tiles left over from a building project—they created a small home that is perfect for their needs. This is becoming more commonplace, as people opt to decouple themselves from stuff, and simplify their lives.

The tiny house trend has caught the interest of so many people who wish to reduce their environmental footprint and embrace simpler living, that it has practically become a movement. Living more simply and having fewer material possessions has led people to consider downsizing the spaces they live in. The movement is, therefore, about more than just living in smaller spaces.

Its roots can actually be traced all the way back to 8,000 B.C., when people first lived, cooked, and had toilet areas inside round clay houses with thatched roofs. Several thousand years later, Mongolian yurts appeared. Famously, in 1845, Henry David Thoreau wrote a meditation on living simply and "deliberately" while being surrounded by nature in a one-room cabin on Walden pond. Jay Shafer spearheaded the modern movement when he built a tiny house, and wrote a book about it in 1999 (D'Silva, 2022).

Why Live in a Tiny House?

For those who wish to have a lower environmental footprint, tiny house living is a match made in heaven. These houses cost much less to build than conventional ones, and use much less energy—around 20-30% of that of most homes in the U.K., for instance (D'Silva, 2022). They can be fitted out with solar and wind power, enabling owners to live off grid. They are economical, portable, eco-friendly, community-minded, and frequently mortgage-free. They may also be rented or owned. Perhaps everyone should live in one?

Tiny houses measure around 100–400 square feet in size, as opposed to the average American house size of 2,600 square feet (The Tiny Life, 2018). To understand how big (or small) that is, 100 square feet is equivalent to a cabin on a cruise ship. Those with an adventurous spirit might prefer something with wheels, like a campervan or converted bus, but others are happy to have a house on a firm foundation.

Most tiny houses are independent structures, parked on a large lot with other buildings or on a property with a larger home. Other owners rent space in caravan parks or camping grounds by the month, and move around. If you opt to stay in one place for some time, these monthly rentals can add up. It can also be costly to move tiny houses around: A truck and trailer will be needed at the very least. Do your research and ensure that your house isn't too wide to travel if you aim to be nomadic, or opt for a wheeled option.

Some houses are custom-built by the owners, while others are purchased, adapted from trailers, or built using a tiny house kit.

There are endless variations on the theme, but all have the same principle: simpler living in a smaller space.

One of the potential pitfalls with tiny home ownership—especially if you want to own land—are the costs of buying property. Buying a plot of land and developing a tiny house can be challenging. Some people get around this by putting their tiny house on property owned by family members, while others rent land cheaply from farmers, which also enables them to avoid the need for planning permissions (in the U.K. at any rate, it is very difficult to get planning permission for tiny houses). Another work-around is to purchase land and then change the land-use to glamping or a small farm.

Things are slightly more advanced in the U.S., where around 10,000 people own tiny homes (D'Silva, 2022). Architects are even starting to specialize in designing tiny houses, as the trend accelerates across the nation. There are some caveats, however: You can't build a tiny house wherever you wish, and mortgage lenders won't approve loans for them.

For some, having a tiny house seems very restrictive. Most people who are part of the movement opt for very small dwelling places for environmental reasons. Others do it out of financial concerns. And still, others like the idea of freedom and having more time to do the things they want.

It goes without saying that having a tiny house makes your money go much further, especially when you consider that most Americans spend a third to half of their earnings on their homes. A mortgage represents a 15 year investment on average, and the costs of maintenance and upkeep, insurance, repairs, and improvements are one of the reasons why many Americans are living from payday to payday (The Tiny Life, 2018). Owning a house costs far more than you would expect.

If you're wanting to adopt a minimalist lifestyle, owning a large house might be counterproductive, as they consist of large spaces that will inevitably be filled with furniture and other material possessions. One of the big advantages of a tiny house is that your overhead expenses are generally much lower than those for larger buildings, and they're easier to maintain. You may need to pay insurance and land rental, but it's still far less than regular home ownership costs. If you have a wheeled home, you also have the ability to move to another location without too much hassle.

The tiny house movement has enabled people to find a simpler way to live. Tiny houses are part of a broader system where individuals and society as a whole are looking for ways to address the problems we are experiencing in the modern world today. Benefits include having a smaller environmental footprint, greater financial freedom, and a sustainable life.

Who is More Likely to Own a Tiny House?

If you're thinking about downsizing to a tiny house, here are a few statistics to help you with your decision. For starters, 68% of tiny house owners have no mortgage, compared with nearly 30% of average American homeowners. Seventy-eight percent of people who live in tiny houses own their own homes, compared to the national average of about 65% of people living in traditional houses. About a third of tiny house owners are over 50, so this might be a great retirement option (The Tiny Life, 2018). More women own tiny houses than men, seeking independence and hassle-free lifestyles. Tiny house owners also save more, and have more funds to invest. By far the majority of tiny house owners do not have any credit card debt, and are more likely to have a college degree.

In the U.S., the tiny house market is dominated by young professionals who want to get out of the city—or at least have a country retreat. Most builders aim to live in their tiny house full-time, while others use them as holiday homes, or rent them out. Sustainability is very high on the agenda of those drawn to the tiny house movement, as these houses have a particularly low carbon footprint.

Since the pandemic, the movement has exploded, as everyone wants to get out of the city and into the country. After spending so much time in isolation and online, people are seeking time out in the physical world, looking for offline connections. In the U.K. some investors and developers are considering lifestyle estates made up of tiny houses. Some developments include facilities like zero-waste shops, eco-laundrettes, and communal kitchen and dining areas. Eco-villages with temporary and permanent tiny house options are also being considered.

Key Takeaways From the Tiny House Movement

As we've seen, the tiny house movement is embracing the principles of minimalism and zero waste. Here are some of the things we can learn from those who have opted for smaller dwellings, whether we live in a regular house, or are considering moving into a much smaller one:

- Get rid of clutter before moving into your new home. Even if we don't consider ourselves hoarders, many of us have more possessions than we need. If you're moving into a tiny house, you can't possibly take it all, hence the need to declutter before moving. Even if you are simply moving from one conventional apartment or house to another, it's a good idea to declutter before you move. Take a long look at your closets, storerooms, basements, and outbuildings. Donate or give away anything you haven't used for at least six months—chances are, you won't miss them. Start reducing your possessions gradually in the months before you move. Don't keep all your sentimental items; just keep those that are particularly important. Try and keep the number of keepsakes below ten.

- Remember that bigger isn't always better, despite what the marketers and advertising gurus would have us believe. As we've mentioned previously, larger spaces tend to come with higher costs. Consider how little space you need to make you happy.

- If you're transitioning to a tiny house, it's imperative to try out smaller spaces before you build to avoid feeling claustrophobic, or facing impracticalities when you actually move in. The internet is filled with stories of people struggling to make up double beds in tiny lofts, having closets the size of crawl spaces, and nowhere to snuggle with a good book when the weather is wet or cold. Go to open houses, model homes, and even your friends' or relatives' houses, and see how they feel. Take a careful look at small spaces, like bathrooms, powder rooms, and laundry rooms. Decide what is "too small" for you.

- Make sure that most rooms can be used for a range of different activities. Use your guest bedroom as an office, or turn your laundry room into a crafting space or mudroom. If you want a formal dining room to enhance your home's resale value, turn it into a den, or make it a place where your children can do their homework.

- Eliminate any unused, unfurnished space in your home. These don't really add value to your life. Talk to your designer or architect about ensuring that all the space is usable. Even a stairwell can be turned into a walk-in pantry, a storeroom, or even a small greenhouse (if it is on the outside of your house).

- Use your vertical space. If you have high ceilings and long walls, add bookshelves you can use for storing things. Put up extra shelving in places like your garage, the laundry room, kitchen, or bathroom. Use hooks and pegboards to make the most of vertical spaces.

- Expand your living area to the great outdoors. If you live in a warm climate, chances are you're doing this anyway. Tiny house dwellers need to make the most of outdoor living spaces to avoid feeling cramped or cooped up. In cooler weather, use firepits and outdoor heaters to stay warm.

- Add a loft. These can provide additional living spaces, and can be used for children's bedrooms or office space if you work from home. Turn it into a game room or home theater, or even an additional guest room.

- Most people want beautiful kitchens—and this is often the first room in a house to receive a makeover. But kitchens should also be designed for cooking (after all, that's what kitchens are used for). Opt for efficient workstations and minimal appliances, focusing on what you really need. This excludes hobby chefs, by the way, who might have more appliances and fancy cookware than the rest of us. Cluttering up your kitchen with trendy, oversized appliances you will rarely use, if ever, isn't the best use of your space or your money, either.

One of the primary reasons people opt to go minimalist and zero waste is environmental concerns, be they biodiversity loss, carbon emissions and climate change, reducing pollution, preserving natural resources, using more eco-friendly products, or saving orangutans in tropical rainforests. Find out how adopting these lifestyles can reduce your impact on the Earth.

Chapter 9:
How Minimalism and Zero Waste Living Helps Save the Planet

If you've ever completed a personal ecological footprint or carbon footprint calculator, the results probably came as a surprise to you. Even if you're an avid recycler and do your best to avoid plastic, the calculator might have thrown up things such as carbon emissions, exacerbated if you own your own vehicle, or use coal-fired electricity. Perhaps you don't buy as much secondhand stuff as you think you do, or you have succumbed somewhat to the fast fashion trend. Embracing a minimalist and zero waste lifestyle can certainly help to reduce your planetary footprint.

As we've discussed in some detail in this book, living with less is not only a goal for personal happiness and freedom, it's also extremely good for the planet. Reducing carbon emissions at the household level is important, as 60% of global greenhouse gas emissions are a result of household consumption (Wright, 2020). This isn't just the obvious things like transport and food, but also purchased products, where carbon was emitted during production. Citizens in developed countries emit more greenhouse gasses than those in the developing world but, as those nations catch up, humanity's global carbon footprint grows. Of course, increasing consumption, as you'll likely know from personal experience, doesn't necessarily make one happier, and it's a big reason for the move toward minimalist, zero waste lifestyles.

The things that truly make us happy, in fact have virtually no material value attached to them—like being out in nature, getting creative, having good relationships, and a sense of purpose and belonging all fulfill us in ways that material possessions can never do.

People in the U.K. who have chosen to live low-consumption lives have done so mainly because of environmental concerns. Both as individuals and as a society, if we focus more on things that promote our well-being, rather than material possessions and consumption, the world would likely be a much better place.

Minimalism, zero waste, and sustainability are inextricably linked, and all contribute to saving the planet. If a zero waste culture were to become the norm, for instance, Earth's natural resources, which are being used up at an alarming rate, would be conserved. Mining, logging, and other forms of extraction use significant amounts of energy, and are often highly polluting. About 50% of people in the U.S. depend on groundwater, but the supply is being depleted faster than it can replenish itself in many parts of the country (Global Conscious, n.d.). This is an indication that the need for natural resources has already started outstripping demand. A zero waste mindset considers how natural resources can be preserved, and ensures that outputs can be either reused, repaired, or recycled. This reduces both energy consumption and pollution.

Adopting a zero waste culture would help to reduce environmental pollution, much of which is "out of sight, and out of mind." But it is happening. Did you know, for example, that 1.2 trillion gallons of untreated sewage and stormwater, together with industrial wastewater, are dumped into U.S. freshwater supplies every year? If everyone aimed to reduce, reuse, repair, and recycle, there would be less pollution.

Both zero waste and minimalist lifestyles require less manufactured goods, which would reduce environmentally damaging human activities. This would include mining and logging, where energy-intensive extraction is necessary to supply the escalating demand for products.

And that's not all. Zero waste in particular promotes the circular economy. This offers social benefits, as well as being eco-friendly, in that more jobs are created, and local and regional economies are boosted. Local waste, composting, and upcycling facilities would be built to cater for a new "zero waste" economic system. As more local salaries are put back into the community, a more prosperous local economy arises as a result. In addition, zero waste communities are more united, and enjoy different forms of social support. There could be projects and workshops promoting sustainability via the distribution of used materials, as well as cleaner air and water supplies. All strata of society would benefit from a zero waste culture.

Similar to zero waste, a minimalist lifestyle automatically encourages eco-friendly living. Here are some of the key ways in which it does:

- Buying less stuff automatically means that there is less stress on natural systems. This also reduces the need for more production, automatically saving on resources such as minerals, natural ingredients, chemicals, and more. If we don't buy things in the first place, this means less needs to be produced. And, if everyone lived like a minimalist or "zero waster," our landfills wouldn't need to be so enormous.

- As a minimalist, anything that doesn't contribute to our needs or serve us in any way should be given away, or passed on to someone who could use it. This prevents them from ending up in a landfill because we don't want them any more, or can't use them. Giving or donating our surplus stuff also contributes to the circular economy.

- Minimalists and zero wasters are more conscious of what they consume. When a fast food restaurant throws a lot of unwanted plastic cutlery, napkins, and sauce sachets into the bag, we wonder why this was necessary. Minimalists refuse plastic bags at the grocery store, and repurpose or repair existing items rather than buying new ones.

- Buying less means that when we do buy, we are able to invest in quality items that last longer, and are recyclable and repairable. For example, if we buy a quality appliance that lasts ten years, this is better for the environment than buying an endless stream of appliances that need replacing every six months. In the latter case, poor quality means that more appliances need to be produced, using more planetary resources, and generating more waste.

Using Less and Saving Environmental Resources

While this book—and minimalism and zero waste in general—have tended to focus on material possessions, there are other ways people can embrace these lifestyle options in order to conserve Earth's precious, and diminishing, natural resources. Some of the major natural resources that sustain the planet—and are also used by people—include animals, plants, water, coal, oil, minerals, timber, land, light, soil, and energy. Natural resources can either be renewable (e.g. solar and wind energy, biomass energy, and hydropower) or nonrenewable. The latter cannot always be replenished as fast as they are used up due to growing demand for them. These include water, fossil fuels, natural gasses, minerals, and nuclear energy.

Humanity—and in fact all life on Earth—cannot survive without natural resources. Our basic needs like water, air, food, and shelter are all derived from nature, and must be conserved. Another problem we face is that using nonrenewable resources, such as fossil fuels, is responsible for climate change and global warming. By conserving natural resources, we can both reduce greenhouse gas emissions and ensure the survival of human beings and all the other creatures that share the planet with us.

Fresh Water

Believe it or not, freshwater is actually very scarce on Earth, despite it covering around 70% of the planet's surface. Only 3% of the world's water is in fact freshwater, with as much as ⅔ locked up in glaciers or otherwise unavailable. This means that around 1.1 billion people globally do not have ready access to fresh water. The human population has also grown exponentially over the last 50 years, which has transformed aquatic systems throughout the world, with 41% of humanity living in river basins that are under water stress (World Wildlife Fund, n.d.).

Because human water use is increasing exponentially, much of the water systems that maintain ecosystems, or are used for growing food crops, are becoming stressed. Water sources are either drying up or becoming too polluted to use, and over half of the world's wetlands have disappeared (World Wildlife Fund, n.d.). Agriculture both consumes and wastes vast amounts of water. Climate change is also affecting rainfall distribution worldwide, further reducing water availability.

The problem is being exacerbated by pollution, including untreated sewage, industrial wastewater, and pesticides and fertilizers that leach from farms with runoff. Pollutants have even reached underground aquifers in some regions, making the groundwater unusable, which is a big problem for people who live in water-scarce parts of the globe.

Agriculture uses around 70% of the world's freshwater on average, but much of this is wasted due to faulty irrigation systems, inefficient application methods, and cultivating crops in climates and regions for which they are not suited (World Wildlife Fund, n.d.). These practices are emptying the world's rivers, lakes, and underground aquifers. Many countries that produce the majority of the world's food are operating at full capacity in terms of available water. This means that there is very little spare capacity to weather meteorological events such as severe droughts.

Some countries in sub-Saharan Africa are already feeling the effects of the double whammy of climate change impacts and scarce water resources in drier climates. In 2018, the city of Cape Town in South Africa hit the headlines when a multi-year drought emptied dams, reservoirs, and catchments, affecting untold numbers of people (Tucker, 2020). The city eventually had to open up natural springs fed by aquifers beneath Table

Mountain in an effort to assist thirsty citizens, and draconian water restrictions were introduced.

Researchers at Stanford University and the National Oceanic and Atmospheric Administration (NOAA) have concluded that such extreme events will become the norm in many parts of the world by the end of this century. This is due largely to climate change—and the prediction is that, although Cape Town averted disaster, mega-droughts like the one experienced in 2018 could impact the region two or three times a decade (Tucker, 2020). The researchers also found that other parts of the world with similar climates could experience their own Day Zeroes in coming years. Rainfall deficits—like the one that affected Cape Town—come with a slew of economic and social impacts. For instance, farmers faced losses of around $400 million as crop yields plummeted, and tens of thousands of agricultural jobs were lost (Tucker, 2020).

Largely as a result of human development, about half of the world's wetlands have disappeared since 1900 (World Wildlife Fund, n.d.). Wetlands are among the most productive ecosystems, supporting an array of animals, birds, and plants, and providing rice, an important global staple. They also filter water, control floods, protect human settlements from storms, and provide recreational opportunities.

Carbon Emissions

Emissions of Earth-warming greenhouse gasses, including carbon dioxide and methane, are contributing to climate change–and individuals and households are contributing to it as well. In 2018, the average U.S. person's carbon footprint was a staggering 18.3 tons a year. In order to hold global temperature increases to 35°F or less, everyone on the planet will need to have an average annual carbon footprint of less than 2 tons (Cho, 2018).

Conserving Natural Resources at Home

There are several ways people can conserve natural resources, a practice that fits in well with the principles of minimalism and zero waste:

- Use less water. Take shorter showers, use low-flow showerheads, and turn off the faucet while you brush your teeth. All these simple acts can allow you to save water every day. Only use dishwashers or washing machines when there is a full load, and switch to energy-saving appliances wherever possible.

- Turn off lights and electronics such as the television when you leave a room, or have finished watching. Unplug appliances when they are not in use, as they can still consume electricity when plugged in. Switching to LED lighting, which requires less wattage than standard bulbs, can also save electricity.

- If you can, switch to renewable energy resources whenever possible. Use solar panels or install a wind turbine on your property to harvest these natural, renewable energy sources. This can reduce our reliance on natural gas or coal-fired power over time.

- Turn down your thermostat. Heating and air conditioning account for about half your electricity bill, but lowering the heat by just two degrees in winter can help conserve energy in your home. Raising it by two degrees in summer will also help reduce your monthly bills (Cho, 2018).

- Shop at thrift stores. Buying secondhand clothing can reduce the amount of reusable clothing that ends up in landfills by extending its lifecycle. This also increases the amount of time between the use of a garment and its disposal.

- Change your diet to include more fruits, vegetables, grains, and beans. Start with meatless Mondays and go from there.

- Wash your clothing in cold water, using cold water detergent. Doing two loads of laundry in cold water can save up to 500 pounds of carbon dioxide a year (Cho, 2018).

- Drive less. Instead, walk, use public transport, rideshare, carpool, or cycle to your destination whenever possible. When driving, avoid unnecessary braking and acceleration to reduce fuel consumption. Take care of your car to ensure maximum fuel efficiency. When running errands, combine them to reduce your driving. Use less air conditioning when driving, open the windows, and turn on the cruise control on longer trips.

- Fly as little as possible. If you must, fly non-stop, as this uses less aviation fuel.

- As mentioned previously in this book, refusing, recycling, reusing, repairing, and upcycling your stuff can also save on planetary resources.

Conclusion

Sustainable living is the latest buzzword for those wishing to live lighter on the planet. The sustainable lifestyle has many facets, from embracing renewable energy to using less planetary resources, and even reconsidering your diet. In this book, I have focused on minimalism and zero waste as starting points for those wishing to embrace a more eco-friendly way of life.

Modern Western society is essentially very wasteful. Most people consume things they don't need, and are slaves to consumerism and fads. Clever marketing and advertising ploys encourage this by tapping into common human needs and desires, cultivating the lie that, by buying certain products and services, our psychological and social needs will be met. This started as early as the end of World War I, when knowledge about the human psyche was used to manipulate people into swapping consumption and possessions for relationships and meaning. People have been misled into believing that the more they buy, the happier they will be, but the opposite is often the case.

However, there are a number of things that individuals and communities can do to counter planetary destruction as a result of our materialistic society. Minimalism essentially aims to reduce clutter, and epitomizes buying and consuming less in order to embrace a more meaningful life focusing on the things that are important to us, rather than buying more stuff that needs to be maintained. Less becomes more, as we buy only what we need, and avoid any extraneous stuff that does not contribute to our happiness and well-being. This means we have more time for one another, more time to build relationships, be creative, pursue rewarding hobbies, read good books, and spend time in nature. These provide a healthy sense of fulfillment, as it was meant to be.

The zero waste movement is similar but the focus is on reversing our wasteful habits and aiming to send as little (preferably nothing) to landfill as possible. Zero wasters are supporters of the circular economy, and are encouraged to reduce, reuse, recycle, repair, repurpose, and compost waste. Some zero wasters make only one jar of trash a year. Many waste items, from old clothing to tin cans, old furniture, fabric scraps, and plenty else can be reused in our homes and offices. All it takes is a little creativity.

Social projects such as the tiny house movement and the buy nothing project encourage us to live on less, live debt-free, and give away surplus items we don't want or even use—our talents, abilities, and free time—to the benefit of our communities.

Going minimalist and zero waste is also beneficial for the

environment. It saves on scarce resources because reduced demand for stuff means less production and manufacturing, less extractivism, less carbon emissions, and less pollution. All this enables natural systems and raw materials to last longer, sustaining life as we know it, and ensuring that we do not experience scarcity in an age of apparent plenty.

So start taking small steps to decouple yourself from the lure of materialism. Declutter your home one room, or perhaps one closet, at a time. Start recycling, reusing, and repairing broken items. Buy quality essentials that will last. Stop supporting fast fashion. Switch to sustainable cosmetic brands. Use less plastic. Spend more time in nature. Join the Buy Nothing movement and give your unwanted items, or your time, to others in your community.

No one is an island. Embrace community and neighborliness rather than rampant individualism based on what money can buy—or the status you believe possessions may confer on you. Go for a walk. Get a pet. Take up birdwatching. Spend more time with friends. Re-establish connections with people, nature, and the world. You will find yourself enjoying a richer, more rewarding existence than you ever thought possible.

Finding Motivation

We all have different motivations for making eco changes in our lives. For some, it is a logical drive to sustain the next generation, or an emotional response to ease our own conscience about our wastefulness. After learning about revealing truths and Western excesses, some may physically respond with a knot in their gut to change. Some are spiritually driven by their belief and faith in God. Others believe that God provided us with the Earth and gave people dominion over it, that is, to steward it well. Being pro-stewardship is not a command to love plants and animals more than people, but to value personal belongings less and instead value the Earth more, which was a gift to all.

Regardless of your motivations, the phrase that fits is: Whoever is not against us, is for us. Let's be for each other, and work together toward a sustainable and healthy future.

Remember To Leave a Review

Finally, if you enjoyed reading this book and found it helpful, remember to leave a review. As an independent author with a small marketing budget, reviews are my livelihood on this platform. If you enjoyed the book, I'd really appreciate it if you left your honest feedback. I love hearing from my readers and I personally read every single review.

References

Addison County. (2019). *Top five reasons to compost - ACSWMD.* ACSWMD. www.addisoncountyrecycles.org/food-scraps/composting/101/why-compost

Alex. (2022, April 20). *World toilet paper consumption,* Mapped. Vivid Maps. www.vividmaps.com/toilet-paper-consumption

Arria-Devoe, A. (n.d.). *Ordering takeout the sustainable way.* Goop.com; Goop Inc. www.goop.com/wellness/environmental-health-civics/how-to-reduce-takeout-plastic/

AZ Quotes. (n.d.). *Kenneth E. Boulding quotes about growth.* AZ Quotes. https://www.azquotes.com/author/23449-Kenneth_E_Boulding/tag/growth

Baum, I. (2022, January 19). *This is what those best-by, sell-by, and use-by dates really mean.* Allrecipes. https://www.allrecipes.com/article/best-by-sell-by-use-by-dates/

BBC News. (2021, August 4). *Thailand bans coral-damaging sunscreens in marine parks.* BBC News. https://www.bbc.com/news/world-asia-58092472

Becker, J. (2019, November 13). *Minimalism: 8 essential principles of a simple lifestyle.* Www.becomingminimalist.com. https://www.becomingminimalist.com/what-is-minimalism/#:~:text=MINIMALISM%20IS%20OWNING%20FEWER%20POSSESSIONS

Boman, E. (2019, September 26). *Making food delivery more accessible and sustainable.* Uber Newsroom. https://www.uber.com/en-AU/newsroom/making-food-delivery-more-accessible-sustainable/

Brosnahan, T. (n.d.). *Site of Thoreau's house on Walden pond.* Newenglandtravelplanner.com. Retrieved September 19, 2022, from https://newenglandtravelplanner.com/go/ma/boston_west/concord/sights/thoreau_hse_site.html

Cecilia. (2020, September 27). Mining Mica - The True Costs Of Beauty Products -. The Sustainability Project. https://thesustainabilityproject.life/blog/2020/09/27/mining-mica/#:~:text=Environmental%20Impact%20of%20

Mining%20Mica&text=The%20creation%20of%20ope
n%20pits

Center for Sustainable Systems. (2021). *U.S. environmental footprint factsheet.* Center for Sustainable Systems. https://css.umich.edu/publications/factsheets/sustaina bility-indicators/us-environmental-footprint-factsheet#:~:text=With%20less%20than%205%25%20 of

Cernansky, R. (2021, September 16). *Beauty has a waste problem, and it's not packaging.* Vogue Business. https://www.voguebusiness.com/sustainability/beauty-has-a-waste-problem-and-its-not-packaging

Cho, R. (2018, December 27). *The 35 easiest ways to reduce your carbon footprint.* State of the Planet. https://news.climate.columbia.edu/2018/12/27/35-ways-reduce-carbon-footprint/

Constable, H. (n.d.). Your brand new returns end up in landfill | BBC Earth. Www.bbcearth.com. https://www.bbcearth.com/news/your-brand-new-returns-end-up-in-landfill

Cox, J. (2021, October 28). *Economic growth rate slows to 2% on a sharp slowdown in consumer spending.* CNBC.

https://www.cnbc.com/2021/10/28/us-gross-domestic-product-increases-at-2point0percent-annualized-pace-in-q3-vs-2point8percent-estimate.html

Cross, D. T. (2018, September 19). *A nifty idea: a biodegradable water bottle made from algae*. Sustainability Times. https://www.sustainability-times.com/green-consumerism/a-nifty-idea-a-biodegradable-water-bottle-made-from-algae/#:~:text=J%C3%B3nsson%20has%20combined%20a%20powdered

The Daily Gardener. (2020, August 2). *21 Ingenious DIY compost bin ideas you can try*. The Daily Gardener. https://www.thedailygardener.com/diy-compost-bin-ideas

DocuWiki (2022, February 4). *The party's over: How the West went bust*. https://docuwiki.net/index.php?title=The_Party%27s_Over:_How_the_West_Went_Bust

D'Silva, B. (2022, January 4). *Why the tiny house is perfect for now*. Www.bbc.com. https://www.bbc.com/culture/article/20211215-why-the-tiny-house-movement-is-big

Durrani, A. (2020, August 19). *Can you recycle that? Here's what the recycling numbers on plastic mean.* Real Estate News & Insights | Realtor.com®. https://www.realtor.com/advice/home-improvement/recycling-numbers-plastic/

Earley, B. (2021, February 16). *Going green? The pros swear by these homemade cleaning solutions.* Oprah Daily. https://www.oprahdaily.com/life/g30666676/homemade-cleaners/

Eartheasy. (2019). *Zero waste: a beginner's guide.* Eartheasy Guides & Articles. https://learn.eartheasy.com/guides/zero-waste-a-beginners-guide/

Eco.Logic (n.d.). Eco.Logic. *What does food waste have to do with climate change?* Retrieved August 31, 2022, from https://www.ecologicprograms.org/blog/foodwasteproblem?utm_source=google?utm_medium=cpc?utm_campaign=lp?utm_content=131860674939?utm_term=food%20waste%20in%20the%20us&gclid=Cj0KCQjwio6XBhCMARIsAC0u9aH5_1Gmr6gkwuiyhDBVjHHY0ib9WSIxnv3b7IMZFpTrDwjk_7whOmEaAqt-EALw_wcB

EcoTree. (2021, September 13). *What is greenwashing and why is it bad?* EcoTree. https://ecotree.green/en/blog/what-is-greenwashing-and-why-is-it-bad#:~:text=Greenwashing%20is%20bad%20for%20many%20reasons.%20The%20most

EDN Staff. (2022, March 29). *Fact Sheet: Single Use Plastics* | Earth Day. Earth Day. https://www.earthday.org/fact-sheet-single-use-plastics/

Ellis, J. S. (2019, April 9). *Transitioning from consumerism to minimalism.* John Spencer Ellis: Digital Nomad, Location Independent Business. https://johnspencerellis.com/transitioning-from-consumerism-to-minimalism/

Fenton, L. (2022, August 15). *Everything you ever wanted to know about Buy Nothing groups.* Real Simple. https://www.realsimple.com/home-organizing/green-living/buy-nothing-groups

Gem. (2021, March 4). *Minimalism versus consumerism: how to find the right balance for you.* Decluttering Ideas. https://declutteringideas.com/minimalism-versus-consumerism/

Gifford, D. (2014, October 26). *30 ways to use less paper.* Small Footprint Family™. https://www.smallfootprintfamily.com/30-ways-to-use-less-paper

Global Conscious. (n.d.). *Answered: The environmental benefits of zero waste explained.* Global Conscious. Retrieved September 6, 2022, from https://globe-conscious.com/benefits-of-zero-waste/

Global Footprint Network. (2016). *Earth overshoot day* - Global Footprint Network. Footprintnetwork.org. https://www.footprintnetwork.org/our-work/earth-overshoot-day/

Gregory, C. (2016). *Internet addiction disorder - signs, symptoms, and treatments.* PsyCom.net - Mental Health Treatment Resource since 1986. https://www.psycom.net/iadcriteria.html

Guillard, V., Gaucel, S., Fornaciari, C., Angelier-Coussy, H., Buche, P., and Contard, N. (2018). *The next generation of sustainable food packaging to preserve our environment in a circular economy context.* Frontiers in Nutrition, 5(121). https://doi.org/https://doi.org/10.3389.fruit.2018.0012

Hall, M. (2021, June 6). *Bubble wrap recycling and disposal.* Business Waste. https://www.businesswaste.co.uk/bubble-wrap-recycling-and-disposal/

Haynes, T. (2018, May 1). *Dopamine, smartphones and you: a battle for your time.* Science in the News; Harvard University. https://sitn.hms.harvard.edu/flash/2018/dopamine-smartphones-battle-time/

Heritage Paper. (2016, June 29). *Pros and cons of biodegradable packing peanuts - Heritage Paper.* Heritage Paper. https://www.heritagepaper.net/pros-and-cons-of-biodegradable-packing-peanuts/

Hutchings, C. (2018, April 21). 20 *Easy sustainable swaps to reduce waste | 20 eco-friendly life hacks.* The Edgy Veg. https://www.theedgyveg.com/2018/04/21/20-easy-sustainable-swaps-reduce-waste/

IANS. (2022, August 25). *Explained: Ethereum set for mega "merger" to become more energy efficient.* Business Standard India. https://www.business-standard.com/article/markets/explained-ethereum-set-for-mega-merger-to-become-more-energy-efficient-122082500670_1.html

ICT Works. (2020, February 20). *Digital technologies are part of the climate change problem.* ICTworks. https://www.ictworks.org/digital-technologies-climate-change-problem/#.YwksGXZBzcs

In Pictures: How much plastic are you eating? (2020, December 11). Www.aljazeera.com. https://www.aljazeera.com/gallery/2020/12/11/in-pictures-how-much-plastic-are-you-eating

Johnson, B. (n.d.). *About Bea. Zero waste home.* https://zerowastehome.com/bea/

Kellogg, K. (n.d.). *About zero waste.* Going Zero Waste. https://www.goingzerowaste.com/zero-waste-1/

Kellogg, K. (2020, April 9). *What is zero waste? What is the circular economy?* Going Zero Waste. https://www.goingzerowaste.com/blog/what-is-zero-waste-what-is-the-circular-economy/

Kelly, M. L. (2021, November 30). *What's the environmental impact each time we hit "buy now," and can we change course?.* NPR.org. https://www.npr.org/2021/11/30/1060185929/what-s-the-environmental-impact-each-time-we-hit-buy-now-and-can-we-change-cours

Krieger, A. (2019, July 16). *Are bioplastics better for the environment than conventional plastics?* Ensia. https://ensia.com/features/bioplastics-bio-based-biodegradable-environment/

Law, B. (2021, April 26). *How do people make paper out of trees, and why not use something else?* The Conversation. https://theconversation.com/how-do-people-make-paper-out-of-trees-and-why-not-use-something-else-156625#:~:text=Did%20you%20know%20that%20it

Lotzof, K. (2020, October 7). *Your mobile phone is powered by precious metals and minerals.* Www.nhm.ac.uk.

Lowe, L. (2019, September 20). *What thrift stores want you to know before you make a donation.* TODAY.com. https://www.today.com/style/what-thrift-stores-want-you-know-you-make-donation-t162979

Maiti, R. (2020, January 29). *Fast fashion: its detrimental effect on the environment.* Earth.org. https://earth.org/fast-fashions-detrimental-effect-on-the-environment/

Mauch, C. (2016) *Introduction: The call for zero waste.* RCC Perspectives, 3(3), 5–12. https://www.jstor.org/stable/26241370#metadata_info_tab_contents

Marsh, J. (2022, January 31). *The fast fashion environmental impact.* Environment Co. https://environment.co/the-fast-fashion-environmental-impact/

Massimi, J. (2014, October 19). *The 7 tactics of hidden persuaders.* Nurture Development. https://www.nurturedevelopment.org/blog/the-7-tactics-of-hidden-persuaders/

Masterclass. (2021a, June 7). *How to conserve natural resources: 8 conservation tips.* Masterclass. https://www.masterclass.com/articles/how-to-conserve-natural-resources

Masterclass. (2021b, June 7). *How to go zero waste - inside the zero-waste lifestyle.* MasterClass. https://www.masterclass.com/articles/zero-waste-lifestyle-explained#9-tips-for-transitioning-into-a-zerowaste-lifestyle

McCarthy, J. (2018, May 14). *The US is rapidly running out of landfill space.* Global Citizen. https://www.globalcitizen.org/en/content/us-landfills-are-filling-up/

McCoy, L. (2021, January 6). *30+ Easy, eco-friendly swaps to make in 2022* - Upjourney. Upjourney.com. https://upjourney.com/easy-eco-friendly-swaps

McDonald, J. (2022, July 13). *Think twice before you throw out your plastic water bottle.* @Dumpstersdotcom. https://www.dumpsters.com/blog/us-trash-production

McVeigh, K. (2021, November 29). *Nurdles: the worst toxic waste you've probably never heard of.* The Guardian. https://www.theguardian.com/environment/2021/nov/29/nurdles-plastic-pellets-environmental-ocean-spills-toxic-waste-not-classified-hazardous

Melina. (2022, January 18). *Your clothes are probably made of plastic: What fabrics to avoid.* Sustainable Rookie. https://www.sustainablerookie.com/fashion/your-clothes-are-made-of-plastic

Montanari, S. (2021, May 20). *Where does your paper come from? The good and the bad news.* Popular Science. https://www.popsci.com/environment/paper-products-sustainability/

National Geographic. (n.d.). *Smart plastics guide.* https://www-tc.pbs.org/strangedays/pdf/StrangeDaysSmartPlastics Guide.pdf

Nayar, J. (2021, August 12). *Not so "green" technology: the complicated legacy of rare earth mining.* Harvard International Review. https://hir.harvard.edu/not-so-green-technology-the-complicated-legacy-of-rare-earth-mining/

Nelson, M. (n.d.). *Big lessons we can learn from the tiny house movement.* Elemental.green. Retrieved September 6, 2022, from https://elemental.green/big-lessons-we-can-learn-from-the-tiny-house-movement/

Ofei, M. (2022, August 12). *What is minimalism? An introduction to living with intentionality.* The Minimalist Vegan. https://theminimalistvegan.com/what-is-minimalism/

Okafor, J. (2021, October 8). *Environmental impact of cosmetics & beauty products.* TRVST. https://www.trvst.world/sustainable-living/environmental-impact-of-cosmetics/

Olivia. (2020, July 4). *Top 10 upcycling ideas* | Flora & Fauna. Www.floraandfauna.com.au. https://www.floraandfauna.com.au/blog/top-10-upcycling-ideas

O'Mara, M. (2021, March 26). *How much paper is used in one day?* Record Nations, Shred Nations. https://www.recordnations.com/2016/02/how-much-paper-is-used-in-one-day/

Paper on the Rocks. (n.d.) *We want to bring balance.* Paper / on the Rocks. https://paperontherocks.com/mission

Plastic Oceans International (2018). *Facts about plastic.* Help - Plastic Oceans Foundation. Plastic Oceans International. https://plasticoceans.org/the-facts/

Plastic Pollution Coalition. (2022, January 25). *The ugly side of beauty: the cosmetics industry's plastic packaging problem.* Plastic Pollution Coalition. https://www.plasticpollutioncoalition.org/blog/2022/1/25/the-ugly-side-of-beauty-the-cosmetics-industrys-plastic-packaging-problem

Plastic Soup. (n.d.). *Plastic is everywhere: in water, air and soil.* Plastic Soup Foundation. Retrieved August 23, 2022, from https://www.plasticsoupfoundation.org/en/plastic-problem/plastic-soup/plastic-is-everywhere/#top

Poor, A. (2019, January 14). *Top 6 environmental threats caused by digital electronics | HPE.* Www.hpe.com. https://www.hpe.com/us/en/insights/articles/top-6-

environmental-threats-caused-by-digital-electronics-1901.html

Proud. (n.d.). *What are reduce, reuse, recycle, repair and upcycle?* Proud. https://proudofficials.com/en/news-article/reduce-reuse-recycle-repair-upcycle

Rai, V. (2019, December 28). *Unseen 2019: The ugly side of beauty waste*. Livemint. https://www.livemint.com/mint-lounge/features/unseen-2019-the-ugly-side-of-beauty-waste-11577446070730.html

Reichardt, I., & Frayne, M. (2011). *Essential organics - The essence of organic gardening*. Forrest Publications. (Original work published 2008)

Rojas, I. (2012, September 21). *What's wrong with tree plantations?* Mongabay Environmental News. https://news.mongabay.com/2012/09/whats-wrong-with-tree-plantations/

Rosane, O. (2021, October 5). *Carbon footprint of computing and ICT may be bigger than expected, study says*. Treehugger. https://www.treehugger.com/computing-emissions-worse-than-thought-study-5204571

Rostamian, M. (2021, October 20). *Zero waste skincare gifts to solve beauty's plastic problem.* LIVEKINDLY. https://www.livekindly.com/zero-waste-beauty-plastic-problem/

Sager, J. (2019, January 24). *Don't toss that! 11 surprising things you can recycle.* Realtor.com. https://www.realtor.com/advice/home-improvement/surprising-things-you-can-recycle/

Science History Institute. (2016, December 20). *The history and future of plastics.* Science History Institute. https://www.sciencehistory.org/the-history-and-future-of-plastics

Scott, M. (2017, April 24). *What you need to know about consumerism.* Swiftmoney.com. https://swiftmoney.com/blog/what-you-need-to-know-about-consumerism/#:~:text=Consumerism%20has%20a%20good%20and

Seema. (2019, November 25). *Food waste is not garbage! -* Trash Hero World. Trash Hero World. https://trashhero.org/food-waste-is-not-garbage/?gclid=CjwKCAjw4JWZBhApEiwAtJUN0FQ

AbG00bbMOC25lJ9f_lhAIj1cakK9cLJEHuCsSNBoyI
5v9GmccEhoCdUAQAvD_BwE

Simpson, K. (2019, July 24). *51 Simple swaps you can make to go plastic free.* The Green Hub. https://thegreenhubonline.com/plastic-free-zero-waste-swaps-to-reduce-plastic-waste/

Sky News. (2021, November 25). *Coastline litter decreasing - but plastic still making up majority of beach waste, study suggests.* Sky News. https://news.sky.com/story/coastline-litter-decreasing-but-plastic-still-making-up-majority-of-beach-waste-study-suggests-12477469

Smith, L. (2020, April 6). *The disposable society: an expensive place to live.* *Investopedia.* https://www.investopedia.com/articles/pf/07/disposablesociety.asp

Sort It Out Sustainably. (2021, January 9). *5 Environmental benefits of minimalism.* Www.sortitoutsustainably.com. https://www.sortitoutsustainably.com/blog/the-5-environmental-benefits-of-minimalism

SOS Future. (2020, June 16). *How to compost at home?* Sos Future. https://sosfuture.org/blogs/news/how-to-compost-at-home?gclid=CjwKCAjw4JWZBhApEiwAtJUN0GqHZ

-

dmZ8HHIftEb_YTrgKEevKqU5qAi7MTvex87yJrNx7
KaPL6jRoC-gUQAvD_BwE

Sustainable Jungle. (2020, February 2). *What is sustainable living?* Sustainable Jungle. https://www.sustainablejungle.com/sustainable-living/what-is-sustainable-living/

Taub, B. (2021, April 28). *Humans are using 173 percent of Earth's resources each year.* IFL Science | Nature. https://www.iflscience.com/humans-using-173-percent-earths-resources-each-year-59540

Thompson, C. (2021, June 2). Swedish dishcloth review: An eco-friendly paper towel. CNN Underscored. https://www.cnn.com/cnn-underscored/reviews/swedish-dishcloth-cellulose-sponge

The Tiny Life. (2018). What is the tiny house movement? Why tiny houses? | The Tiny Life. The Tiny Life. https://thetinylife.com/what-is-the-tiny-house-movement/

Tiseio, I. (2022, May 31). Paper demand globally 2020-2030. Statista.

https://www.statista.com/statistics/1089078/demand-
paper-globally-until-
2030/#:~:text=The%20global%20consumption%20of
%20paper

Tucker, D. T. (2020, November 9). Cape Town's "day zero"
drought a sign of things to come. Stanford News;
Stanford   University.
https://news.stanford.edu/2020/11/09/cape-towns-
day-zero-drought-sign-things-
come/#:~:text=Cape%20Town%20never%20actually
%20reach

University of Alberta. (2013). What is sustainability? In McGill
(p.   1).   University   of   Alberta.
https://www.mcgill.ca/sustainability/files/sustainabilit
y/what-is-sustainability.pdf

Up Journey Editors. (2021, January 6). 30+ Easy eco friendly
swaps to make in 2022 - UpJourney. Upjourney.com.
https://upjourney.com/easy-eco-friendly-swaps

U.S. EPA. (2013, April 18). Preventing wasted food at home.
Www.epa.gov.
https://www.epa.gov/recycle/preventing-wasted-food-
home

Vanderlinden, C. (2022, July 12), *What you need to know about bokashi composting*. The Spruce. https://www.thespruce.com/basics-of-bokashi-composting-2539742

Velez, H. (2022, June 7). 99 Sustainable swaps to incorporate into your daily routine. The Good Trade. https://www.thegoodtrade.com/features/sustainable-living-tips

Wang, H. (2014, July 9). The end of the era of heavy fuel oil in maritime shipping. International Council on Clean Transportation. https://theicct.org/the-end-of-the-era-of-heavy-fuel-oil-in-maritime-shipping/

The World Counts. (2020). State of the planet: number of consumers. Theworldcounts.com. https://www.theworldcounts.com/challenges/planet-earth/state-of-the-planet/number-of-consumers

World Food Programme. (2020, June 2). 5 Facts about food waste and hunger. World Food Programme. https://www.wfp.org/stories/5-facts-about-food-waste-and-hunger#:~:text=One%2Dthird%20of%20food%20produced

World Wildlife Fund, Australia. (2021, July 2). The lifecycle of plastics. Wwf.org.au. https://www.wwf.org.au/news/blogs/the-lifecycle-of-plastics

World Wildlife Fund. (n.d.). Water scarcity | Threats | WWF. World Wildlife Fund. https://www.worldwildlife.org/threats/water-scarcity

Wright, L. (2020, January 16). Can a minimalist mindset help save the planet? | DW | 06.01.2020. DW.COM. https://www.dw.com/en/can-a-minimalist-mindset-help-save-the-planet/a-51733322

Young, O. (2022, March 2). The environmental impact of cosmetics is tremendous—here's why. Treehugger. https://www.treehugger.com/environmental-impact-of-cosmetics-5207672

Zero Waste Scotland. (2019, December 1). What is the circular economy? Zero Waste Scotland. https://www.zerowastescotland.org.uk/circular-economy/about

Image References

The image, *Waste Pyramid* was provided by B.R. Pohl

Printed in Great Britain
by Amazon